MERDE
ENCORE!

MERDE ENCORE!

GENEVIÈVE

**Illustrated by
MICHAEL HEATH**

**"Les beaux gestes" drawings by
ARTHUR FILLOY**

ATHENEUM   New York   1987

Atheneum
Macmillan Publishing Company
866 Third Avenue, New York, N.Y. 10022

Library of Congress Cataloging-in-Publication Data

Geneviève.
  Merde encore!

  Text in English and French.
  1. French language—Slang—Glossaries, vocabularies, etc. 2. French language—Conversation and phrase books—English. I. Title.
  PC3741.G38 1987   447   87-24123
  ISBN 0-689-11938-0

Macmillan books are available at special discounts for bulk purchases for sales promotions, premiums, fund-raising, or educational use. For details, contact:

Special Sales Director
Macmillan Publishing Company
866 Third Avenue
New York, N.Y. 10022

10 9 8 7 6 5 4 3 2 1

Printed in the United States of America
First American Edition

*Aux copains chez Angus & Robertson
(le dirlo Barry et sa nana Cindy,
Murray, Helen, Janet, Roz & Jill),
à mon jules et mes mômes*

CONTENTS

INTRODUCTION

Before reading this book, you should have digested or at least nibbled at the contents of its predecessor, *MERDE! The REAL French You Were Never Taught at School*. It's not just that I want you to buy both books ("cela va sans dire"), but I shall at times in this book assume knowledge acquired in the first.

To give newcomers to our linguistic venture a hint of the value of our previous study, think of the importance of possessing "merde" in your vocabulary. People who have changed the course of history have used it, so why should you lose out on such great moments as when Napoleon told Talleyrand, "Vous êtes de la merde dans un bas de soie" (You're shit in silk stockings)? Surely you know of the moment of the word's apotheosis when General Cambronne, having been called upon to surrender at the battle of Waterloo, yelled it out to the British forces, thus immortalizing the five-letter word known ever after as "le mot de Cambronne."

Now, if you enjoyed *MERDE!* and, with it, finally broke the code of those French conversations which had always eluded you, restricted as you were to the French you were fed at school, you will have appreciated the fact that language is not just an accumulation of words but also a key to the spirit and to the character of the people who speak it. You will also, I hope, have had a good laugh in the process. What I offer here is further exploration of colloquial vocabulary and idioms and, through them, deeper insights into the French psyche. French idioms are often very funny, based as they are on concrete and colorful imagery. I'll give you a few examples just to arouse your interest.

Picture this: **"enculer les mouches,"** a priceless image. As you may remember from *MERDE!*, that translates as "to fuck a fly's ass," an image meaning "to nitpick, to split hairs," but how much more colorful than the English translation. So there will be elements of scatology in this book (hurray!), but you must learn to accept that urino-anal imagery, so frequently used by the French, is not necessarily rude. For example, there are two perfectly ordinary and acceptable names for colors which are in the above-mentioned genre:

1. **"couleur caca d'oie"** means literally the color of goose shit yet is a normal description for a yellowish-green hue, and if Zola can use it in his books, why shouldn't it be part of your vocabulary?

2. **"une couleur pisseuse"** (literally, a urinelike color) means a wishy-washy, insipid color.

One more splendid expression, while we're on the subject, to illustrate the concrete nature of many French idioms: **"autant pisser dans un violin"** (literally, one might as well piss in a violin) is used to express frustration, lack of progress, banging one's head against a brick wall. Finally, to show that the visual brilliance of French idioms does not depend merely on excretion: **"sucrer les fraises"** (literally, to sugar the strawberries) describes someone, usually an old person, who has the shakes. Can't you just picture the movement of a hand shaking sideways as it would when sprinkling sugar over strawberries?

I
VERBS:
The nouvelle conjugaison

(Well, not nouvelle to the Frogs, but probably nouvelle to you)

THE MOI-JE SYNDROME

The French like emphasis in speech. This has meant that single pronouns have been found wanting. Therefore, one finds the use of double pronouns, particularly in the first persons singular and plural where this need to underline, allied to French egocentricity and mania for individualism, has given rise to the **moi-je** syndrome:

Moi, j'aime pas ce mec. (I don't like that guy.)

Moi, je suis contre. (I'm against it.)

Moi, je vais te foutre mon poing sur la gueule. (I'm going to punch your face in.)

Special attention needs to be paid to the first person plural, which, you have learned, is "nous." So it still is, but it has been subverted by the now ubiquitous "on," which has graduated from being the indefinite third person singular pronoun ("on dit que" = it is said that) to being the second half of the double pronoun, "nous, on." Worse, the agreement of participle or adjective is with the first person plural, even if "nous" is left out and the verb itself is in the third person singular:

Nous, on est dégoûtés. (We're disgusted.)

Avec les copains, on est allés au cinoche. (We went to the flicks with some pals.)

Disgusting, say the grammar purists! (Mr. Grammar Purist, ever heard of the ostrich or the dodo?)

So, for a final look, an example for each pronoun:

Moi, je suis belle, intelligente et cultivée. (I'm pretty, intelligent and cultured.)

Toi, t'es un pauvre con. (You're a pathetic idiot.)

Elle, elle est moche comme un pou. (She's very ugly, as ugly as sin; she's a dog.)

Nous, on en a marre. (We're fed up.)

Vous, vous êtes des emmerdeurs. (You're all pains in the ass.)

Eux, ils sont débiles. (They're idiots, they're stupid.)

CODE CONJUGATIONS

To make patronizing jokes about clodhopping peasants or Africans as they often do, to their great amusement, the French have "code" conjugations of which you should be aware, otherwise you'll miss the reference (try reading *Tintin au Congo* without such knowledge). The joke-peasant says "j'avions," "j'étions," and "je vas" and is prone to answering a question with "'têt ben qu'oui, 'têt ben qu'non" (in other words, "peut-être bien que oui, peut-être bien que non" = maybe yes, maybe no; maybe it is, maybe it isn't). Meanwhile, in "petit nègre" (pidgin French), the first person singular is "moi y'en a" plus an infinitive, as in "moi y'en a vouloir" (I want); "moi y'en a pas être" (I'm not). The articles "le" and "la" become "li," and "monsieur" becomes "missié." Hence, one could have "Missié Tintin, moi y'en a pas avoir vu li chien Milou" (I haven't seen your dog Milou, Mr. Tintin), or "moi y'en a vouloir toi donner fusil" (I want you to give me the rifle).

II
SUFFIXES:
Instruments of contempt and belittlement

So you think that suffixes are just another boring little grammatical item? Not in French, where some are invested with great power. The French, with their superiority complex, make much use of suffixes to express contempt and belittlement. Here are the basic ones, with a few examples of each (and once you have mastered them, you can coin your own words).

For belittling, meet monsieur –(a)illon:

un avocaillon (from "avo-
   cat" = lawyer)   a small-town lawyer

un curaillon (from "curé"
   = priest)   a village priest

un moinillon (from
   "moine" = monk)   an inconsequential monk

un criticaillon (from "cri-   a two-bit critic
  tique" = critic—literary,
  artistic, etc.)

un écrivaillon (from "écri-   a hack writer
  vain" = writer)

Meet his many offspring: −(a)iller, −(a)illerie, −(a)illeur:

discutailler (from "discu-   to quibble
  ter" = to discuss)

la politicaillerie (from "la   petty politics
  politique" = politics)

un rimailleur (from   a poetaster
  "rime" = rhyme)

Meet monsieur −ton:

un chèqueton (from   a check
  "chèque" = check)

un naveton (from "un   a third-rate work of art
  navet" = a third-rate
  work of art)

un cureton (from "curé"   a village priest
  = parish priest)

For contempt, meet monsieur −ard and madame −arde:

un(e) banlieusard(e)   a suburbanite
  (from "la banlieue" =
  the suburbs)

snobinard(e) (from   snooty
  "snob")

un politicard   a politico

froussard(e) (from "la   yellow-bellied, scaredy-cat
  frousse" = fear)

un(e) **soulard(e)** (from "soûl = drunk")	
	a lush, drunk, boozer
un(e) **soiffard(e)** (from "soif" = thirst)	
un(e) **fêtard(e)** (from "la fête" = a good time)	a hell-raiser
un(e) **bondieusard(e)** (from "le bon Dieu" = God)	an excessively, narrow-mindedly pious person

For underlining a point, meet monsieur et madame **–issime,** who can be used to emphasize positive as well as negative qualities, depending on what they are tagged on to:

nullissime (from "nul")	totally useless, worthless
gravissime (from "grave")	extremely serious
rarissime (from "rare")	very rare
richissime (from "riche")	phenomenally rich, loaded

7

III
LES BEAUX GESTES:
French sign language

Platitude: the French gesticulate when they speak. Revelation: they are not always just flapping around; some gestures are a language of their own and need translation. Be very attentive and practice in front of your mirror. (All instructions are given for right-handers; left-handers should adapt them accordingly.)

1. Va te faire foutre!

The king of gestures, known as "le bras d'honneur" (literally, gesture of esteem, respect, homage—a supreme irony). Absolutely vital in all situations, especially when driving.

Meaning: Get stuffed! Up yours! Fuck you!

Method: Right arm stretched out, smack your left hand palm down on the right arm, just above the elbow, making the forearm spring sharply upwards.

2. J'en ai ras le bol.

Meaning: I've had it up to here, I'm fed up.

Method: Using your right hand, palm facing downward, trace a quick line from left to right, level with your eyebrows or across the top of your head.

3. Quelle barbe! Qu'est-ce qu'il/elle est rasoir!

Meaning: What a bore, what a drag! What a bore he/she is!

Method: Loosely bend the fingers of your right hand, then stroke your right cheek up and down with the back of your fingers, between the first and second joints.

4. Barrons-nous!

Meaning: Let's get the hell out of here!

Method: Both hands flat, palms facing downward, smack the back of the right hand with the left palm.

9

5. Y'a quelqu'un qui a un verre dans le nez!

Meaning: Someone's had too much to drink!

Method: Form an "o" with the fingers of your right hand, making a very loose fist. Put it in front of your nose, facing straight ahead, and make a turning, screwing motion right to left (90 degrees will do).

6. Mon oeil!

Meaning: My eye! My foot!

Method: Pull the skin below your right eye downward, using only your right index finger.

7. Aïe, aïe, aïe, aïe, aïe!

Meaning: Uh oh, someone's in trouble!

Method: Right hand palm facing your chest, fingers apart, shake it loosely up and down.

10

8. C'est pas donné!

Meaning: It ain't cheap, it'll cost you.

Method: Right hand palm facing upward, straighten fingers upward and rub thumb up and down the top of the other grouped fingers.

9. J'm'en fous!

Meaning: I don't give a damn!

Method: Right hand out, palm facing upward, make a hitting motion toward your shoulder.

10. Alors, là!

Meaning:
1. I really don't know.
2. I doubt it can be done.

   Method: Raise both hands toward your shoulders, palms outward. Lower lip should protrude and eyebrows rise.

11. Cocu! (An overworked and much favored insult.)
Meaning: Cuckold!
Method: Stick your two index fingers up on either side of your head, like horns, and wiggle them up and down (horns being the traditional symbol of the cuckold).

12. Au poil! Super! Fantastique!
Meaning: Great! Terrif! and so on.
Method: Makes a "thumbs up" sign with your right hand, and stamp it down slightly in front of you.

Note that the gesture of thumbing one's nose at someone is called **"faire le pied de nez à quelqu'un"** or **"faire la nique à quelqu'un."**

IV
GUILLOTINED FRENCH:
From aristo to socialo

Read the following:

Napo détestait les intellos.

Le sous-off est complètement parano.

C'est l'intox à coup de gégène.

Le PDG adore la BD.

À la manif, y'avait beaucoup d'écolos rachos.

Mysterious? Well, the clues will appear shortly. Someone who has been guillotined is said in French to have been "raccourci(e)," that is, shortened. This is what happens to many French words. The guillotine effect is widespread in conversation and in media vocabulary. It is most often found in words that have, in their original form, an interior "o" (usually in the penultimate or ante-penultimate syllable), that "o" becoming the last letter of the guillotined word. Learn five words a day.

un(e) écolo (écologiste)   an ecologist (à la Green-peace or the Green movement)

un(e) collabo (collaborateur, –trice)	a collaborator (the French World War II version)
folko (folklorique)	quaint, out-of-date, folksy
rétro (rétrograde)	said of someone or something that indulges in nostalgia, is old-fashioned, or imitates a style of the past (**"une mode rétro," "une politique rétro"**)
maso (masochiste)	masochistic
porno (pornographique)	porno
un(e) aristo (aristocrate)	an aristocrat
une diapo (diapositive)	a slide, a transparency (photography)
le croco (crocodile)	crocodile leather, as in **"un sac en croco"** = a crocodile-skin bag
une leçon de géo (géographie)	a geography lesson
un labo (laboratoire)	a lab
un mélo (mélodrame)	a dramatic scene, as in **"faire tout un mélo"** = to act up, to make a big scene
un chrono (chronomètre)	a stopwatch
parano (paranoïaque)	paranoid

14

un(e) **toxico** (toxicomane)	a drug addict
mégalo (mégalomane)	megalomaniac (a common French trait)
l'édito (m.) (l'éditorial)	the editorial
la météo (les prévisions météorologiques)	the weather forecast

Many words just have the "o" added to their shortened state:

un(e) **intello** (intellectuel, –le)	an intellectual
un(e) **socialo** (socialiste)	a socialist
un(e) **facho** (fasciste)	a fascist
un(e) **coco** (communiste)	a commie
un(e) **prolo** (prolétaire)	a prole
un **dico** (dictionnaire)	a dictionary
un(e) **invalo** (invalide)	an invalid
racho (rachitique = literally, suffering from rickets)	skinny, scrawny
le, la **proprio** (propriétaire)	the landlord, landlady
le **frigo** (frigidaire)	the fridge

Or else they are simply left in their guillotined condition:

| **réac** (réactionnaire) | reactionary |

15

la fac (faculté)	the university faculty
le bac (baccalauréat)	the baccalaureate
la rédac (rédaction)	the essay (a school assignment)
l'occase (occasion)	the opportunity
la pub (publicité)	advertising, the advertisement
le bénef (bénéfice)	the profit
la manif (manifestation)	the demo
un trav (travelot, travesti)	a transvestite, drag queen
un(e) mac (un maquereau/ une maquerelle)	a pimp/a madam
cap (capable)	able ("**T'es cap de le faire?**" = Do you dare do it? Do you think you can do it?)
l'alu(m). (aluminium)	aluminum
un macchab (macchabée)	a stiff (corpse)
le Boul'Mich (Boulevard St. Michel)	(that street in the heart of the Latin Quarter)
le sous-off (sous-officier)	the NCO (noncommissioned officer)

l'**intox** (intoxication)	brainwashing
le, la dirlo (directeur, directrice)	the director (the boss)
le gégène (général)	the general (army officer)
la gégène (génératrice)	torture by electric shock (do not confuse with the above "*le* gégène")
le PDG (Président-Directeur-Général)	the boss of a company
la BD (bande dessinée)	the comic strip

A special note on "la BD": this is a new art form to which much time, discussion, cogitation, and ink are devoted. It is a thriving industry, and there is even an annual BD festival at Angoulême. To you and me, it is just a comic strip but, as it exists in France, where things must be given a more serious—dare I say intellectualized—bent, it is a boom industry—whoops, art form. French children hardly seem to read books anymore unless they are in BD form, and adults have their own, including porno ones, for their delectation.

Translation of introductory sentences:

Napoleon hated intellectuals.

The NCO is absolutely paranoid.

It's brainwashing by electric torture.

The boss is crazy about comic strips.

The demo was full of scrawny ecology types.

17

V
COUNTING IN FRENCH:
Some numbers are more equal than others

"Je n'étais qu'un zéro qui, en chiffre, signifie quelque chose quand il y a un nombre devant lui."

Cardinal de Richelieu
(the number before his zero being Louis XIII)

UN, DEUX, TROIS . . .

Some numbers are more favored than others in French, as they are part of commonly used idioms. Before you are introduced to them, learn these few colloquial words for things often counted.

les berges (f.)
les piges (f.)
years, as in **"C'est un vieux gaga, il a eu quarante piges hier."** = He's an old geezer; he was forty yesterday.

les bornes (f.)
kilometers, as in **"J'ai roulé cent bornes."** = I drove a hundred kilometers.

les balles (f.)	francs, as in **"File-moi quinze balles."** = Give me fifteen francs.

Zero is very important, as it quantifies, in the usual negative French way, one's esteem for someone or the level of an activity. We'll start on the other side of zero and move up from there:

c'est un minus	he/she is a nitwit
il est nul **elle est nulle** **c'est une nullité**	he/she is useless, stupid
il/elle est nullissime	he/she is totally useless, stupid
c'est un zéro	he/she is a nothing, a complete nonentity
alors, là, c'est zéro pour la question!	no way, certainly not!
avoir le moral à zéro	to be depressed, to be down in the dumps
s'en foutre de quart comme du tiers	not to give a damn
à un/deux doigt(s) de . . .	on the verge of, as in **"à deux doigts de la mort"** = at death's door
en moins de deux	very quickly

19

en deux temps trois mouvements en deux coups de cuiller à pot	in two shakes of a lamb's tail
se retrouver/tomber les quatre fers en l'air	to fall flat on one's back (the image is that of the horse on its back with its shoes ["fers"] up in the air)
un de ces quatre (matins)	one of these days
tiré(e) à quatre épingles	dressed to the nines
faire ses quatre volontés	to do as one pleases, without taking others into account
ne pas y aller par quatre chemins	to get straight to the point, not to beat around the bush
se plier en quatre pour quelqu'un	to put oneself out for someone, bend over backward for someone
couper les cheveux en quatre	to split hairs, nitpick
dire ses quatre vérités à quelqu'un	to give someone a piece of one's mind

ne pas casser quatre pattes à un canard	to be not worth writing home about, to be unexciting (literally, not to break the four legs of a duck)
il y avait quatre pelés et un tondu	there was only a handful of people there (literally, there were only four baldies and one short-back-and-sides)
les cinq lettres	euphemism for "merde"
en cinq sec	very fast, in a jiffy
le mouton à cinq pattes	the impossible, the unattainable
vingt-deux, voilà les flics!	look out, here come the cops!
se mettre sur son trente et un	to wear one's Sunday best
voir trente-six chandelles	to see stars (literally, to see thirty-six candles, after being punched, for example)
je m'en fous comme de l'an quarante	I don't give a damn (literally, I don't care about it any more than I do the year 40)
un soixante-neuf	a "soixante-neuf" (*that* 69, you know!!!)

faire les cent pas	to pace up and down
s'emmerder à cent francs de l'heure	to be bored to tears
attendre cent sept ans	to have a long wait

VOIR TRENTE-SIX CHANDELLES = TO SEE STARS

faire les quatre cents coups	to get into lots of trouble, to lead a dissipated life
je te/vous le donne en mille	you'll never guess

THE FROGCLOCK

In the seventies, a marvelous slogan was coined that summed up the drudgery and routine of the Parisian worker's life: **"métro-boulot-dodo"** (remember from *MERDE!* that "boulot" means work or job, and "dodo" is baby talk for sleep: "métro" [the subway] is the form of transport used daily to get to work). By setting out the daily routine we get the Frogclock:

7:00 café;	2:00 boulot;
7:15 caca et un brin de toilette;	(5:00–7:00 baise);
	7:00 métro;
8:00 métro;	8:00 bouffe et télé;
8:30 boulot;	(11:00 baise);
Noon bouffe;	Midnight dodo.

A quick reminder that "caca" = crap (baby talk but used by adults too), that "bouffe" = grub, food. What's the "brin de toilette"? Nothing to do with "caca"; it means a quick wash (and, in France, that *means* quick . . . see chapter VIII). What about this "baise" (screw) twice a day? The expression **"faire un petit cinq-à-sept"** refers to adulterous sex enjoyed between the end of office hours and the return to the conjugal domain, where marital sex can be had at the later hour. Speaking of fornication, you should know that **"un baise-en-ville"** is a woman's overnight bag owing its name to its original purpose: to contain the necessary items for an illicit quickie in town in the days when contraception required bulkier items than the odd pill. Variation for the young male adolescent: subtract the "baise" and add a 6:30 "branle" (masturbate), replace "boulot" with "bahut" (school) and add another "branle" before "dodo."

A few other times should be noted, as they appear in idioms:

faire passer un mauvais quart d'heure à quelqu'un	to give someone a rough time (literally, to make someone go through a rough fifteen minutes)
les trois quarts du temps	most of the time
un bouillon d'onze heures	a poisoned drink
chercher midi à quatorze heures	to complicate things unnecessarily

Apply your knowledge:

1. Si Lucrèce Borgia en avait marre de quelqu'un, elle ne cherchait pas midi à quatorze heures; elle lui filait un bouillon d'onze heures et en deux temps trois mouvements son compte était fait.

2. Le concert ne cassait pas quatre pattes à un canard; d'ailleurs il n'y avait que quatre pelés et un tondu.

3. Il est tellement nullissime qu'il faut attendre cent sept ans pour qu'il finisse le boulot qu'un autre ferait en cinq sec.

1. If Lucrezia Borgia got fed up with someone, she didn't make a big deal out of it; she just slipped him/her a poisoned drink and in no time at all his/her number was up.

2. The concert was nothing to write home about; anyway there was hardly a soul there.

3. He is so totally useless that it takes him forever to finish a job that someone else would do in no time at all.

VI
SOUND EFFECTS:
Gurgle, splash, hiccup!

You don't imagine that the French go "ah-choo" or say "wow," do you? The latter is almost a physical impossibility for them, the letter "w" not really being French (there are very few words starting with "w" in French dictionaries and they are mostly taken from English). To approximate the "wow" sound, it has had to be transcribed as "ouaouh" or, left to its own devices, it would have come out as "vov." Anyway, if you want to understand conversation or liven up your own narrative, you'd do well to learn the following vital sounds.

achoum!	ah-choo
glouglou	gurgle, glug glug
badaboum!	crash!
patatras!	

flac! plouf!	splash!
ouf!	phew!
pouah!	poo! (What a stink!)
miam miam!	yum yum!
toc-toc-toc!	knock-knock-knock!
aïe! ouille!	ow! ouch!
heu, euh ben	um
boum!	bang!
pan pan!	bang-bang! (gunshot)
clac!	smack!
hi, hi	boo-hoo
youpi!	hurray, goody!
taratata!	rubbish, crap
oh là là là là!	uh oh, oh dear! boy oh boy!
patati patata	blah blah blah; yakety-yak
pinpon	siren of a police car, ambulance or fire engine
hic!	hiccup!
guili guili	(the noise the Frog makes when tickling someone)
bôf!	(a sound to accompany the shrugging of shoulders to show indecision, indifference or ignorance)

26

There are certain important nouns and adjectives derived from onomatopoeia:

gnangnan (adj.)   wimpish and given to whining (from the whining sound)

olé olé (adj.)   forward in manner and/or speech; used disapprovingly of such conduct in a young woman (**"Elle est plutôt olé olé, ta copine."** = Your girlfriend comes on pretty strong.)

un scrogneugneu   an old grouch (from the grumbling, grouchy sounds he supposedly emits)

le crincrin   the squeaky, scraping sound of a badly played instrument, particularly a stringed one

le tralala   the frills, the trimmings

faire du tralala   to make a big fuss (when having people over, for example)

les chichis   fuss, ceremony (**"Arrête de faire des chichis."** = Stop making such a big deal of it.)

chichiteux, chichiteuse   affected, lacking in simplicity

A special mention must go to the onomatopoeic **"crac!"** Apart from its sound effect (crack!), the French use it to introduce a dramatic event in a narrative. It is a tool used to emphasize and dramatize. Just before relating the climax of the event, pause, then insert a strong "crac!" and continue your description. Study the following examples.

Ils étaient richissimes et, crac! ils ont tout perdu.
(They were loaded and suddenly they lost everything.)

Ç'avait l'air de bien marcher et puis, crac! on l'a foutu à la porte. (Everything seemed to be going well and then, suddenly, he was kicked out.)

Il me parlait de choses et d'autres et, crac! il m'a embrassée. (He was talking about one thing and another and suddenly he kissed me.)

A few more sentences to test your general ability:

1. Badaboum! Elle tombe! "Aïe, ouille! Hi, hi!" elle se met à pleurer. Un scrogneugneu qui passe lui gueule: "Vous êtes bien gnangnan, vous!"

2. Toc-toc-toc! "Qui c'est?" "C'est la concierge. Faut arrêter votre horrible crincrin, y'a les voisins qui rouspètent."

3. Miam, miam, des frites!

1. Crash! She falls! "Ow, ouch! Boo-hoo!," she starts crying. An old grouch passing by yells at her, "What a little whiner you are!"

2. Knock-knock-knock! "Who is it?" "It's the concierge. Stop scratching that awful fiddle, the neighbors are complaining."

3. Yummy, French fries!

29

VII
THE MOST POPULAR
INGREDIENTS OF
FRENCH IDIOMS:
Food and animals

"Dis-moi ce que tu manges, je te dirai ce que tu es."

A. Brillat-Savarin
(famous gastronome, 1755–1826)

YUM YUM, DRIBBLE DRIBBLE

Here is an appetizer (translations at the end of this section):

1. Oh, dis, hé, arrête d'en faire tout un fromage.

2. C'est pas de la tarte de serrer la cuiller à la viocque: elle sucre les fraises.

3. Alors, mon petit chou, t'es pas dans ton assiette?

4. Occupe-toi de tes oignons, espèce de gros lard.

5. Alors, comme ça, j'ai fait tout ce boulot pour des prunes? La prochaine fois, t'iras te faire cuire un oeuf.

Take a nation of predominantly peasant origin where food has a near-religious dimension, and you are bound to find many idioms based on food imagery, and entertaining they are too. That not very noble vegetable, the cabbage, appears in a number of them, so that's where we'll start.

aller planter ses choux	to retire to the country
entrer dans le chou de quelqu'un	1. to hit someone 2. to knock into, collide with someone
oreilles en feuille de chou	cauliflower ears
bête comme chou	really stupid
être dans les choux	to be in trouble, to be in an awkward situation
faire chou blanc	to fail completely, to draw a blank
chou, choute	cute
mon chou, ma choute	sweetie ("mon chou" can be used for men or women)
avoir du sang de navet	to be spineless, cowardly (literally, to have the blood of a turnip)
les carottes sont cuites	it's all over, all's lost
ne pas avoir un radis	to be broke

avoir un coeur d'artichaut	to be fickle, to fall in and out of love easily, to flirt with everyone one meets
occupe-toi de tes oignons!	mind your own business!
en rang d'oignon	lined up in order of height
le panier à salade	the police van, the paddy wagon
une gourde	a clumsy person
c'est la fin des haricots	it's the last straw
en avoir gros sur la patate	to have a heavy heart about something (une patate = a spud)
une grosse légume	a big wheel, a bigwig
la fraise	the mug (face)
ramener sa fraise	to butt in
sucrer les fraises	to have the shakes
des prunes!	no way!
faire quelque chose pour des prunes	to do something for nothing (i.e. for no reward or without result)
une poire	a sucker, a mug
couper la poire en deux	to meet halfway, to make equal concessions

les bananes	medals, decorations (military)
haut(e) comme trois pommes	tiny (to describe a person)
tomber dans les pommes	to faint
va te faire cuire un oeuf!	go to hell!
quel oeuf!	what a jerk, what a blockhead!
une andouille	a stupid person ("andouille" is a sausage made from chitterlings)
un boudin	a dumpy woman ("boudin" = blood sausage)
ne pas les attacher avec des saucisses ("les" = ses chiens)	to be stingy (literally, not to tie them [one's dogs] up with sausages)
mettre du beurre sur les épinards	to become financially more comfortable, as in "ça mettra du beurre sur les épinards" = that'll make life easier
discuter le bout de gras	to chew the fat, to gab
en faire tout un fromage	to make a big deal out of nothing
défendre son bifteck	to stand up for one's financial interests

être chocolat	to be thwarted, frustrated
casser du sucre sur le dos de quelqu'un	to say things behind someone's back, to badmouth someone
cheveux poivre et sel	salt-and-pepper hair (often used for a distinguished-looking hue)
mettre son grain de sel	to interfere, stick one's two cents in
salé(e)	1. spicy, risqué 2. dirty (of a story, of someone's actions or jokes, etc.)
ça ne manque pas de sel	it's spicy (as above)
un riz-pain-sel	a serviceman (especially an officer) in charge of supplies, a quartermaster
tourner au vinaigre	to go sour (a relationship, for example)
la sauce	torrential rain
la purée de pois	pea-souper (fog)
un gros plein de soupe	a fatso, tub of lard
s'amener comme un cheveu sur la soupe	to come along at an inopportune moment; to be irrelevant (a comment, for example)

être soupe au lait	to have a short temper, to blow one's fuse easily
gratiné(e)	outrageous, extraordinary (actions, stories)
le gratin	the upper crust
c'est du gâteau **c'est de la tarte** }	it's a cinch, it's easy, it's in the bag, it's a piece of cake
c'est pas du gâteau **c'est pas de la tarte** }	it's a tough one, it's going to be rough
tarte (adj.)	silly and ridiculous (describing people or objects, not events)
avoir du pain sur la planche	to have a lot of work ahead, to have a lot on one's plate
se vendre comme des petits pains	to sell like hot cakes
mijoter quelque chose	to cook up something (mischief, a plot, a deal, etc.)
c'est du tout cuit	it's a cinch, it's in the bag
c'est du réchauffé	it's a rehash, it's stale (jokes, arguments, ideas, etc.)
un(e) dur(e) à cuire	a tough, hard person

qu'est-ce que c'est que cette cuisine?	what's all this monkey business?
bouffer (du curé, du politicien, de l'Anglais, etc.)	to hate (priests, politicians, the English, etc.)
bouffer à tous les râteliers	to be a sponger, to cash in on all sides ("râteliers" = dentures, so literally, "to eat from all dentures")
un pique-assiette	a scrounger, a sponger
ne pas être dans son assiette	to be out of sorts (literally, not to be in one's plate)
en faire tout un plat	to make a big production out of something
se serrer la cuiller	to shake hands (literally, to shake each other's spoon—well, remember that in olden days the hand was the eating utensil)
être à ramasser à la petite cuiller	to be in a pathetic state; to be knocked out (a person) (literally, to be in such a state that one can be scooped up with a spoon)
ne pas y aller avec le dos de la cuiller	to act without restraint, to lay it on thick

il/elle n'a pas inventé le	he/she is not very bright
fil à couper le beurre	

Translations of the introductory sentences:

1. Hey, stop making such a big deal out of it.

2. It's not easy to shake hands with the old bag; she's got the shakes.

3. What's the matter, honey, are you out of sorts?

4. Mind your own business, fatso.

5. You mean I did all that work for nothing? Next time you can go to hell.

THAT YUKKY FRENCH FOOD

The French could put you off your food, you know! I'm not just referring to the fact that they eat those frogs' legs (some 200,000,000 frogs are imported for consumption a year), snails (40,000 *tons* eaten a year), calves' brains, and so on, it's the names they sometimes use. If you were given the following menu in a restaurant, you might justifiably feel an urge to go somewhere else. However, what you are about to read are literal translations of perfectly acceptable—indeed, highly appreciated—French comestibles.

MENU DU JOUR
Dribbling-spittle Omelette
Piss-in-bed Salad
Choice of Cheese
(Droppings or The Stinker of Lille)
Nun's Farts
(With Ass-scratcher Jam)
Wine: Pissing Hard

O.K., an explanation is coming! In French, the above items would be as follows (and no Frenchman would bat an eyelid):

Omelette Baveuse
Yes, "baver" means to dribble. The French do not like dry, stiff omelets but runny, squishy ones, so the drooling image refers to the texture of the omelet.

Salade de Pissenlit
You probably know that "pissenlit" is dandelion, but the literal translation cannot be denied. Besides, the Irish call it pissabed (because of its diuretic qualities). Actually, who wants to eat the stuff anyway? Can you imagine any dandelion leaves not having been pissed on by passing dogs?

Crottin
So, "crottin" can be horse or sheep turds; it also happens to be the name of a delightful little goat's cheese.

Le Puant de Lille
This cheese is noted for its strong odor of ammonia, but neither its smell nor its name seems to put consumers off.

Les Pets-de-nonne
Fritters to you and me but what a hilarious image. Actually I'm not so sure that "hilarious" is the right word . . . let's say disgusting, revolting, yukky . . .

Confiture de Gratte-cul
"Gratte-cul" is the haw, or fruit of the wild rose. It seems a shame to give it such an awful name.

Pisse-dru
A Beaujolais brand name.

BON APPETIT!

P.S. You could wash down the exquisite dessert with a sweet Sauterne wine whose particular composition comes from "la pourriture noble" (noble rot), the faint mold that appears on the skin of very ripe grapes when they are bursting with sugar. It is an integral part of the Sauterne winemaking process.

P.P.S. I can't resist adding (and this could be retaliatory ammunition for our Froggy friends) that my dear (English) husband has often asked me to prepare a dessert, the very idea of which I have been unable to stomach because of its repulsive name: spotted dick (ils sont fous, ces Anglais!). I still haven't brought myself to make it.

ANIMALS' NAMES TAKEN IN VAIN

Animal imagery plays a crucial role in the highly colorful expressions of colloquial French, often for negative associations: ugliness, stupidity, stubbornness, or nastiness. The star animals, those with the longest list of appearance in imagery, are inevitably (remembering those peasant origins of the French) domestic or farm animals, so they'll head our list.

avoir un mal de chien à faire quelque chose	to have a hell of a time in doing something
se donner un mal de chien pour faire quelque chose	to bend over backward to do something, to go out of one's way to do something
. . . de chien (e.g. une vie de chien, un temps de chien, un métier de chien)	lousy, rotten, crummy (e.g. a rotten existence, lousy weather, a crummy job)
avoir un caractère de chien	to have a nasty, aggressive disposition
malade comme un chien	as sick as a dog, very ill

AVOIR D'AUTRES CHATS À FOUETTER = TO HAVE OTHER FISH TO FRY

traiter quelqu'un comme
un chien

to treat someone like dirt

mourir comme un chien

to die alone, without anyone to care for one

vivre comme chien et chat	fight like cats and dogs, to bicker constantly
être chien	to be stingy
avoir du chien	to have a certain chic
nom d'un chien!	darn!
faire la rubrique des chiens crevés	to be a journalist confined to reporting lowly, humdrum events (people's dead dogs, petty burglaries)
une vache, une peau de vache, une belle vache, une vraie vache	a hard, nasty, mean person
être vache avec quelqu'un	to be harsh, nasty to someone
c'est vache!	that's too bad, that's rotten
un coup de vache	a dirty, mean trick
manger de la vache enragée	to go through hard times (literally, to eat rabid cow)
une vache à lait	someone who is constantly milked by others, a patsy, a sucker
ça lui va comme un tablier à une vache	it looks awful, ridiculous on him/her (literally, it suits him/her as an apron would a cow)

41

pleuvoir comme vache qui pisse	to rain cats and dogs (literally, to rain like a cow pissing)
parler le français comme une vache espagnole	to speak pidgin French, to murder the French language
mort aux vaches!	down with the cops!
une vache à roulettes	a cop on wheels, a motorcycle cop
un veau	1. a lazy lump of a person 2. a nag (horse) 3. a tanklike car
pleurer comme un veau	to cry one's eyes out
souffler comme un boeuf	to breathe very heavily or with great difficulty
cochon(ne)	dirty (physically or mentally)
eh bien, mon cochon!	well, you devil!
faire un travail de cochon	to make a mess of something
faire un tour de cochon à quelqu'un	to play a dirty, nasty trick on someone
avoir un caractère de cochon	to be a difficult person

hé là, on n'a pas gardé les cochons ensemble!	hey, don't get so familiar! (literally, hey, we didn't keep pigs together)
c'est donner de la confiture à un cochon	it's throwing pearls before swine
être copains comme cochons	to be bosom buddies
des cochonneries ("Il ne raconte que des cochonneries.")	gross or revolting actions, dirty stories (All he tells are dirty stories)
de la cochonnerie ("C'est de la cochonnerie, ces tableaux!")	gargabe, trash (These paintings are a load of garbage!)
les moutons	white horses (the foam on the crests of waves)
les moutons de Panurge	people who follow others blindly, like sheep (Panurge is a Rabelaisian character)
le mouton à cinq pattes	the unattainable, the impossible
revenons à nos moutons	to get back to the subject
jouer à saute-mouton	to play leapfrog
la brebis galeuse	the "black sheep" (literally, the scabby sheep)

la crotte de bique ("Ta bagnole, c'est de la crotte de bique.")	junk, piece of crap (literally, goat droppings) (Your car's a lemon.)
une vieille bique	an old hag
mon biquet, ma biquette	baby, sweetheart, honey-lamb ("biquet" = kid goat)
une cage à lapins une cabane à lapins	a small, badly built dwelling; a rabbit hutch
ne pas valoir un pet de lapin	to be totally worthless (literally, not to be worth a rabbit fart)
c'est du lapinisme!	they have too many children! (reference, of course, to the reproductive capability of the rabbit)
poser un lapin à quelqu'un	to stand someone up
un chaud lapin	a hot-blooded male, a sex maniac
un nid-de-poule	a pothole
une poule mouillée	a scaredy-cat
avoir la chair de poule	to have goose pimples
une cage à poules	a cheaply, badly built dwelling, a chicken coop

se coucher aves les poules	to go to bed very early
avoir la bouche en cul-de-poule	to have pursed lips (literally, to have a mouth shaped like a hen's ass)
quand les poules auront des dents	never in a month of Sundays, when pigs fly (literally, when hens have teeth)
une poule	a tramp, a slut
mon poulet, ma poule	honey, sweetie, etc.
avoir des mollets de coq	to have wiry, skinny legs
sauter du coq à l'âne	to jump from one subject to another
une oie	a jerk
une oie blanche	an innocent, sweet young thing
les pattes d'oie	crow's feet
caca d'oie	greenish-yellow (literally, gooseshit)
ne pas casser quatre pattes à un canard	not to be worth writing home about (literally, not to break the four legs of a duck)
faire un froid de canard	to be freezing cold (weather and temperature only)

WHEN PIGS FLY

QUAND LES POULES AURONT
DES DENTS

un canard	1. a rag (newspaper)
	2. a sugar cube dunked in coffee or a liqueur and immediately eaten
	3. canard (false rumor, hoax)
un pigeon	a sucker, a dupe
se faire pigeonner	to be made a sucker, dupe of
couleur gorge-de-pigeon	a color with iridescent, changing glints as found on the feathers of a pigeon's throat
il n'y a pas un chat	there is not a soul around
il n'y a pas de quoi fouetter un chat	it's not worth making a big deal over (literally, it's not worth whipping a cat over it)
avoir d'autres chats à fouetter	to have more important things to do, to have other fish to fry
le chat, la chatte	the pussy (the female genitals)
appeler un chat un chat	to call a spade a spade
écrire comme un chat	to write illegibly and messily
avoir un chat dans la gorge	to have a frog in one's throat

47

AVOIR UN CHAT DANS LA GORGE = TO HAVE A FROG IN ONE'S THROAT

du pipi de chat	an insipid or watered drink (literally, cat piss)
donner sa langue au chat	to give up (when faced with a riddle)
un âne	a stupid person, a jackass
faire/dire des âneries	to do/to say stupid things
le bonnet d'âne	the dunce's cap
monté comme un âne	to have a big cock, to be hung like a horse

du pipi d'âne	an insipid drink, horse piss
une tête de mule	a stubborn person of limited intelligence
un remède de cheval	a strong medicine that knocks one out, a kill-or-cure remedy
monter sur ses grands chevaux	to get on one's high horse
un grand cheval	a horse (describing a woman)
avoir une fièvre de cheval	to have a raging fever
être à cheval sur (le règlement, par exemple)	to be a stickler for (rules and regulations, for example)
entrer comme dans une écurie	to enter a room, a house, without acknowledging the presence of others
enculer les mouches	to split hairs, to nitpick (literally, to fuck a fly's ass)
tuer les mouches à quinze pas	to have bad breath; to have body odor (literally, to kill flies at fifteen paces)
les pattes de mouche	indecipherable, spidery, tiny scrawl
prendre la mouche	to fly off the handle, to get huffy

quelle mouche te pique?	what's eating you? what the hell's the matter with you?
avoir une araignée au plafond	to have bats in the belfry (literally, to have a spider on the ceiling)
une punaise de sacristie	a narrow-minded old woman who spends lots of time in church (literally, a sacristy bug)

50

une puce	a tiny person ("puce" = flea)
ma puce	term of affection for a small child
secouer les puces à quel-qu'un	to chew someone's ass out; rake someone over the coals
mettre la puce à l'oreille de quelqu'un	to awaken someone's suspicions, to put a bee in someone's bonnet
le pucier	the bed (i.e., the fleabag)
laid(e) comme un pou	very ugly, as ugly as sin (literally, as ugly as a louse)
minute, papillon!	hold it! hold your horses!
pas folle, la guêpe!	I'm/he's/she's nobody's fool! There are no flies on me/him/her ("guêpe" = wasp)

The wild is less well represented, its animals being less familiar than the domesticated ones. However, note:

bander comme un cerf	to have a huge erection (literally, to have an erection the size of a stag's)
ma biche	honey, sweetie ("biche" = doe)

51

avoir une faim de loup	to be ravenously hungry
avancer à pas de loup	to move stealthily
un drôle de zèbre } un drôle d'oiseau }	a weird fellow
un ours mal léché	a clumsy boor
vendre la peau de l'ours	to count your chickens before they're hatched
un chameau	an unpleasant, nasty person
un faisan	a crook, a shark
un vrai panier de crabes	a can of worms, a hornet's nest (figuratively)
un mollusque	an apathetic, dull weakling
une vieille guenon	an ugly old hag ("guenon" = female monkey)
on n'apprend pas à un singe comment faire la grimace	you can't teach an old dog new tricks (literally, you can't teach a monkey how to make faces)
malin comme un singe	very clever
payer en monnaie de singe	to reward with empty promises, with flowery language and nothing more (literally, to pay in monkey money)
laid(e) comme un singe	as ugly as sin

une girafe	a beanpole
une grenouille de béni- tier	a bigoted old woman who spends a lot of time in church (literally, a bap- tismal-font frog)
poisson d'avril!	April fool!

ANIMALSPEAK

No need to tell you that French dogs couldn't possibly go "bow-wow"—imagine, it would come out "bov-vov." If you wish to venture into the animal kingdom or sing "Old Mac-Donald" in French, you'd better learn some appropriate sounds. En France:

le chien fait **ouah ouah,**	le mouton fait **bêêê,**
le chat fait **miaou,**	la vache fait **meuh,**
le canard fait **coin-coin,**	l'âne **hi-han,**
la poule fait **cot-cot-cot- cot-cot,**	le hibou fait **hou hou,**
le coq fait **cocorico,**	la grenouille fait **crôâ crôâ**

Remember especially "cocorico," which is of national sym-bolic importance (see Chapter XI).

How about a few exercises to see how you are doing?

1. "Alors, maintenant, G. Leculgelé va nous présenter la météo." "Oui, eh bien, aujourd'hui, il fera un temps de

chien, il pleuvra comme vache qui pisse et demain, il fera un froid de canard."

2. Dis donc, vieille guenon, quelle mouche te pique?

3. Cet âne, je vais lui secouer les puces, il a encore fait un travail de cochon.

4. Je suis malade comme un chien, j'ai une fièvre de cheval et j'ai la chair de poule.

1. "And now, G. Frozenbutt will give us the weather forecast." "O.K., today it'll be rotten, it'll rain cats and dogs, and tomorrow it'll be freezing."

2. Hey, you old bag, what's eating you?

3. That jerk, I'm going to tell him off, he's made another mess.

4. I'm sick as a dog, I've got a raging fever and goose pimples.

VIII
ANATOMY OF A FROG:
A study of vital organs

No, we're not going to study *that* organ. While not denying its importance, other bits of the anatomy play an equally vital part in the behavior, psyche, pathology and, not least, language of the French.

THE LIVER

Most of you probably don't know the location or function of your liver, but the French are ever aware of its presence and concerned for its well-being. It is an essential part of their obsession with the digestive process—after all, if you have stuffed yourself with food, you have to be sure that it all goes down well. Have you ever suffered from a liver attack? The French do all the time: **"avoir une crise de foie"** is pure indigestion to you and me but, to the French, is more localized. To avoid the dreaded "crise de foie," much care is taken to aid and abet the digestive process. For example, a walk after a meal "pour la digestion" is deemed essential. Once, a French boy on a sailboat paced up and down after lunch, to the amazement of his British hosts; he explained that this was necessary "pour aider la digestion." More conveniently, post-prandial liqueurs are called **"digestifs"** and an Italian one, Fernet-Branca, finds great favor in France because of claims on its label that its mixture of herbs helps digestion—a clever alliance of medicine and pleasure.

Of course, carry the obsession with digestion to extremes, and one has to be concerned with the end product. See a doctor in France about any ailment and it is highly likely that he will ask whether you have been **"à la selle."** This is not a query about your riding ability (as "selle" = saddle, but here used to mean seat) but about your bowel movements. Note the following.

Avez-vous été à la selle aujourd'hui? (Have you had a bowel movement today?)

Comment sont vos selles? (How are your stools? Description of texture and color required, so be prepared.)

Patients may well leave the doctor's bearing a prescription not for our much-prized pills but for a box of suppositories. The French are not pill-poppers but suppository-shovers. Many a naive American or British patient in France has been found munching these waxy pellets in total ignorance of the destined orifice . . . now you know!

Here is some relevant vocabulary:

ça me donne une indigestion	I can't stand it, I'm fed up with it, I've had enough of it (said of any situation)
se faire de la bile	to worry oneself sick (literally, to produce bile, the secretion of the liver)

bilieux, bilieuse	irritable
le spleen	melancholy, the blues (though a different organ, the spleen ["la rate" in French] was also presumed to have an effect on one's moods—particularly the darker ones— and the use of this English word was popularized by Baudelaire in *Les Fleurs du mal*.)

THE NOSE

Listen to two famous Frenchmen:

Pascal: Le nez de Cléopâtre: s'il eût été plus long, toute la face de la terre aurait changé. (Cleopatra's nose: had it been longer, the entire face of the world would have changed.)

Edmond Rostand's character, Cyrano de Bergerac: . . . un grand nez est proprement l'indice/ D'un homme affable, bon, courtois, spirituel,/ Libéral, courageux. (. . . a great nose is truly the sign of a genial, good, courteous, witty, generous and brave man.)

Well, there we are. Don't underestimate the importance of the nose, especially when, like Frenchmen, you are endowed with a—what shall we say?—powerful, imposing one! Apart from its ability to change the course of world history, judge its place in the French view of things by the number of idioms it has . . . nosed its way into:

passer sous le nez de quelqu'un	to miss an opportunity ("Ça m'est passé sous le nez." = I missed the opportunity, it slipped right through my fingers.)
ne pas mettre le nez dehors	not to go outside at all ("Je n'ai pas mis le nez dehors de la journée." = I haven't been out all day.)
avoir le nez fin	to be shrewd
faire quelque chose les doigts dans le nez	to do something with great ease (literally, with one's fingers up one's nose)
mener quelqu'un par le bout du nez	to dominate someone, to do with someone as one pleases, lead him/her around by the nose
ne pas voir plus loin que le bout du nez	to lack foresight, not be able to see past the tip of one's nose
pendre au nez de quelqu'un	to be bound to happen to someone ("Ça lui pend au nez." = He's got it coming to him.)
tirer les vers du nez de quelqu'un	to force someone to tell the truth (literally, to pull the worms from someone's nose)

58

se bouffer le nez	to have a violent quarrel (literally, to bite each other's noses off)
avoir un verre dans le nez	to be tipsy, to have had one too many
fourrer le nez dans les affaires des autres	to stick one's nose into other people's business
se trouver nez à nez avec quelqu'un	to bump into someone
faire quelque chose au nez de quelqu'un	to do something in front of another with impunity and/or cheek, do something right under someone's nose
rire au nez de quelqu'un	to laugh in someone's face
avoir la moutarde qui monte au nez	to get hot under the collar, to lose one's temper (literally, to have the mustard rise up one's nose)

THE TONGUE

Samuel Johnson said that "a Frenchman must always be talking, whether he knows anything of the matter or not." A Frenchman without a tongue is a contradiction in terms. Not only a tool of conversation, the tongue is, of course, used for tasting food and wine, for kissing ("French kissing"), and for having a good gossip (a favorite French pastime). A few idioms:

une mauvaise langue	a gossip
tirer la langue	to be dying of thirst (therefore, one's tongue is hanging out); by extension, to be in great need (do not confuse with **"tirer la langue à quelqu'un"** = to stick one's tongue out at someone)
avoir la langue bien pendue	to be very talkative, to have the gift of the gab
se mordre la langue	1. to hold oneself back from saying something, to bite one's tongue 2. to regret having said something
ne pas avoir sa langue dans sa poche	never to be at a loss for words (**"ce mec n'a pas sa langue dans sa poche."** = that guy's always got something to say.)
donner sa langue au chat	to give up (in games, riddles, etc.)

"LE DERRIÈRE"

If you remember from *MERDE!* the importance of the backside ("le cul" = ass) and of the scatological in everyday vocabulary (knowledge of which is fundamental to the understanding of many a French joke), you will not be surprised to find a number of expressions emanating from that part of the French anatomy:

avoir du cul	to be lucky
l'avoir dans le cul	to be unlucky
avoir quelqu'un dans le cul	to despise someone
en avoir plein le cul	to be fed up with someone or something
en rester sur le cul	to be utterly amazed by something
tirer au cul	to be lazy, to get away with doing as little as possible (gives the noun "**un tire-au-cul**")
avoir du poil au cul	to be brave, gutsy (literally, to have hair on one's ass)
péter plus haut que son cul	to think too highly of oneself (literally, to fart higher than one's ass)
un lèche-cul	an ass kisser
un cul béni	a devout Catholic
un cul terreux	a peasant
avoir chaud aux fesses **serrer les fesses** }	to be scared ("**les fesses**" = butt)

| attraper quelqu'un par la peau des fesses | to catch someone by the scruff of the neck |

OTHER ORGANS: A LINGUISTIC POTPOURRI

Other bits and pieces of the body figure prominently and commonly in idioms, so away we go:

tomber sur un os	to hit a snag
il y a un os	there's a hitch
en avoir par-dessus la tête	to be fed up with someone or something
se casser la tête (à faire quelque chose)	to rack one's brains (doing something)
avoir une tête à claques	to have an unpleasant, stupid, stubborn mien, such that one feels the urge to slap it ("claques" = slaps)
n'en faire qu'à sa tête	to do only as one pleases, to go one's merry way
faire la tête, faire la gueule	to sulk
une tête/une gueule d'enterrement	a long, sad face (literally, a funereal mien)
avoir la tête enflée	to have a swollen, fat head; to be pleased with oneself

avoir une sale tête	to have a nasty, unpleasant look about one
casser la tête (à quelqu'un)	to get on someone's nerves
tenir à un cheveu	to hang by a thread ("**Il n'en tenait qu'à un cheveu.**" = It was touch and go.)
avoir un cheveu sur la langue	to lisp
ça te défrise?	any objection? (literally, does it take the curl out of your hair?)
une grande gueule	a loudmouth
ne pas desserrer les dents	to clam up, to refuse to talk
se casser les dents	to fail
avoir une dent contre quelqu'un	to bear a grudge against someone
avoir la dent dure	to be hard and critical
avoir la dent	to be hungry
avoir les dents longues	to be very hungry
n'avoir rien à se mettre sous la dent	to have nothing to eat (in the house)
être sur les dents	to be overworked

casser les oreilles à quelqu'un	to deafen someone ("**Tu me casses les oreilles avec ta musique.**" = Your music is deafening me.)
ce n'est pas tombé dans l'oreille d'un sourd	it didn't fall on deaf ears
mettre la puce à l'oreille de quelqu'un	to raise someone's suspicions, to put a bee in someone's bonnet
coûter les yeux de la tête	to cost an arm and a leg
s'en battre l'oeil	not to give a damn about something
ne pas avoir froid aux yeux	to be gutsy
tourner de l'oeil	1. to faint 2. to go bad ("**Ta crème tourne de l'oeil.**" = Your cream is going sour. "**Ta plante tourne de l'oeil.**" = Your plant is looking a bit sad.)
avoir quelqu'un à l'oeil	to keep a close watch on someone
ne pas avoir les yeux dans sa poche	to see and notice everything, to have one's wits about one
faire les gros yeux	to scold

COÛTER LES YEUX DE LA TÊTE

$ 10,100

TO COST AN ARM
AND A LEG

65

ça saute aux yeux, ça crève les yeux	it's really obvious
se mettre le doigt dans l'oeil (jusqu'au coude)	to put one's foot in something; to be grossly clumsy or mistaken (literally, to put one's finger in one's eye—up to the elbow).
à l'oeil	free, gratis
taper dans l'oeil de quelqu'un	to click with someone, to hit it off
faire la petite bouche	to turn up one's nose
une fine bouche, une fine gueule	a gourmet
avoir un chat dans la gorge	to have a frog in one's throat
ça m'est/lui est resté dans la gorge	I/he/she found it hard to take, to swallow
jusqu'au cou	completely, seriously ("être dans la merde jusqu'au cou" = to be in deep trouble, "être endetté jusqu'au cou" = to be in debt up to one's neck)
avoir le bras long	to have influence, to have the right contacts

avoir quelqu'un/quelque chose sur les bras	to be saddled with someone/something
gros(se) comme le bras	unsubtle ("**une flatterie grosse comme le bras**" = unsubtle, obvious flattery)
les bras m'en tombent!	I'm amazed, I can't believe it! (literally, it makes my arms fall off!)
être dans les bras de Morphée	to be asleep
j'en mettrais ma main au feu	I am absolutely certain of it, I'd stake my life on it (literally, I'd put my hand in the fire)
ne pas y aller de main morte	not to do something halfway ("**Il n'y va pas de main morte quand il se sert un verre.**" = He sure pours himself a stiff drink.)
prendre quelque chose/ quelqu'un en main	to take charge of something/someone
mettre la main à la pâte	to roll up one's sleeves (literally, to put one's hand to the dough)
faire des pieds et des mains pour faire quelque chose	to move heaven and earth to do something

67

avoir quelque chose sous la main	to have something within arm's reach, at hand
se mordre les doigts	to be impatient, to be annoyed
s'en mordre les doigts	to regret something, to kick oneself for something (an action, a nasty word)
être comme les deux doigts de la main	to be very close (people)
mon petit doigt me l'a dit	a little bird told me
ne pas remuer le petit doigt	not to lift a finger
être à un doigt/deux doigts de la mort	to be at death's door
pouce!	time! (to call a halt to a game, to pause)
se tourner les pouces	to twiddle one's thumbs
un coup de pouce	a little push, i.e. help ("**il lui faudra un petit coup de pouce pour avoir une promotion**" = He'll need someone to put in a good word for him if he's to get a promotion.)
avoir les ongles en deuil	to have dirty fingernails ("le deuil" = mourning)

(être quelque chose) jus-qu'au bout des ongles	(to be something) totally, to one's fingertips (**"Il est socialo jusqu'au bout des ongles."** = He's an out-and-out socialist.)
la Veuve Poignet	masturbation (**"aller voir la Veuve Poignet"** = to masturbate; "la veuve" = the widow, "le poignet" = the wrist)
lever le coude	to be a heavy drinker ("le coude" = the elbow)
se serrer les coudes	to stick together and help one another
jouer des coudes	to elbow one's way
épauler	to give support
donner un coup d'épaule à quelqu'un	to help someone to succeed, to lend someone a helping hand
en avoir plein le dos	to be fed up with something/someone
se mettre quelqu'un à dos	to make an enemy out of someone
avoir bon dos	to be unfairly blamed (**"il a bon dos le train"** = the train makes a good excuse, doesn't it?)

il a une poitrine de vélo	he's a 98-pound weakling
joli comme un coeur	lovely, sweet, cute
prendre/avoir quelque chose à coeur	to take a passionate interest in something
tenir à coeur de quelqu'un	to hold great interest for someone ("**Ce projet lui tient à coeur.**" = He really has his heart set on this project).
loin des yeux, loin du coeur	out of sight, out of mind (notice that emotions feature in the French expression whereas thoughts do in the English)
avoir des haut-le-coeur	to be on the verge of throwing up
avoir quelque chose dans le ventre	to have guts, courage, balls
se mettre à plat ventre devant quelqu'un	to be obsequious toward someone, to crawl, to toady
le bas-ventre	euphemism for the genital area (as in "nether regions")
autant pisser dans un violon	it's a waste of time, there's no point, it's like banging your head against a brick wall

ça lui a pris comme une envie de pisser	he did it out of the blue (literally, he did it as suddenly as a need to piss)
faire des ronds de jambe à quelqu'un	to bow and scrape in front of someone
tenir la jambe à quelqu'un	to buttonhole someone
cela me (te/lui/nous/ vous/leur) fait une belle jambe	a fat lot of good it does me (you/her, him/us/you/ them)
se croire sorti(e) de la cuisse de Jupiter	to think one is God's gift to mankind
être sur les genoux	to be exhausted, to be on one's knees
avoir les chevilles enflées	to be pleased with oneself (literally, to have swollen ankles)
ne pas lui arriver aux chevilles	to be inferior to him/her
faire du genou/du pied	to play kneesies, footsies
prendre son pied	to have an orgasm
bête comme ses pieds	really stupid
(faire quelque chose) comme un pied	(to do something) really badly, clumsily
ça te/vous fera les pieds!	that'll teach you!

se lever du pied gauche	to get out of bed on the wrong side, to start the day off badly
de pied ferme	with determination
partir au pied levé	to leave without adequate preparation ("**partir en guerre au pied levé**" = to go off to war totally unprepared)
mettre les pieds dans le plat	to stick one's foot in it
ne pas savoir sur quel pied danser	1. not to know how to react or what to expect ("**Avec la belle-doche, on ne sait jamais sur quel pied danser.**" = You never know what to expect with a mother-in-law.) 2. to be undecided, to be of two minds
je t'emmerde à pied, à cheval et en voiture	you can go to hell for all I care ("**emmerder quelqu'un**" = to give someone a pain in the ass— remember *MERDE!* The list of forms of transport simply shows the totality of the feeling.)
casser les pieds à quelqu'un	to give someone a pain in the neck

72

FROG PATHOLOGY

MEDICINE

Examine a Frenchman's medicine chest and you will find amazing numbers of medicines, many of which can be bought over the counter. Great faith is placed in the effect of medicine, and the subject animates many a conversation. The French have a high rate of "placebo effect": experiments have shown that 40 percent of French ulcer sufferers were cured by placebos.

HYGIENE

It's *official*: stink-factor, what many foreigners have complained of, the . . . er . . . lack of hygiene of the French, has been confirmed by research! Yes, scientific studies conducted by the French themselves have revealed that the average Frog uses only 2.25 bars of soap a year. If you hear "savon" in a conversation it most likely has nothing to do with soap but with an unpleasant situation: **"passer un savon à quelqu'un"** = to give someone a real telling off, a real piece of one's mind. Now *that* "savon" gets used frequently, you can be sure!

Worse than the news about soap is the revelation that toothbrushes are purchased at the rate of one for every three persons a year! Fifty per cent of them go to bed without brushing their teeth! A *French* journalist wrote recently that many Frenchmen smell like kangaroos kept in cages. French kings' stink is well chronicled: One of the recordholders was Henri IV, whose odor nearly made his fiancée, Marie de' Medici, faint on their first meeting. She had covered her own body heavily with fragrances from her native Italy but they proved an insufficient barrage.

Are the French ashamed of their smell? Not really. Why, many think it is sexy. Napoleon wrote to Josephine from Egypt, where he had been campaigning, "Ne te lave pas, j'arrive." (Don't wash, I'm coming.) Consider, if you will,

73

how many weeks it would have taken for him to arrive back in France . . . if smell was what turned him on, he was in for a good time!

DEATH

The Frenchman's natural irreverence as well as his penchant for drama provide the impetus for a rich vocabulary to convey the notion of death. A news report will not say simply that so-and-so died or passed away but that he disappeared ("a disparu") or left us ("nous a quittés"), as though the fellow had done it on purpose. Announcement of death often takes the form: "Tartempion n'est plus" (so-and-so is no more). Here, then, to express the final voyage:

Sartre n'est plus (present tense only, to announce the event as it happens), **nous a été enlevé, est mort, est décédé, a disparu, nous a quittés, a été rappelé devant Dieu** (well, not applicable to M. Sartre), **a trépassé, s'est éteint, a été emporté** (accompanied by the name of the illness as in "a été emporté par le cancer").

Or, irreverently:

Sartre bouffe les pissenlits par la racine (notice that in English one says *"pushing* up daisies," whereas the French talk of eating), **a cassé sa pipe, a crevé, a clamecé, a claqué, y est resté, a passé l'arme à gauche, a avalé son bulletin de naissance** (swallowed his birth certificate).

So long, buddy!

IX
APPEE BEURZDÉ TOOH YOOH:
Franglais as she is spoke

The good news (for you English-speakers) is that Franglais is expanding daily. If the Frogs go on like this, you won't have to bust your guts trying to learn their language.

The bad news is that you have to learn their funny pronunciation (viz. the chapter heading—Frogpronunciation for "Happy Birthday to You," which is sung up and down the land) as well as the arbitrary gender they give the purloined words. The following is a basic list of real Franglais.

l'after-shave (m.)

le badge

le barbecue

les baskets (= sneakers)

le beefsteack *(sic)*, le bif-
teck

le best-seller

le black-out

le blue-jean

les blues

le bluff

le box-office

le break (= a station
wagon)

le bridge (= dental bridge/
card game)

le bulldozer

le bungalow

le caddy (= the supermar-
ket cart)

le cake (= fruitcake)

la call-girl

le car-ferry

le club

le cocktail

la cover-girl

le cover-story

un crack (= a wizard, an ace)

le dancing

le design

le détective

le discount

le doping

l'escalator (m.)

l'establishment (m.)

le fair-play

les fans

le fast-food

le feedback

le flash

le fuel (heating oil)

le gadget

le gangster

le garden-center

le gay

le gentleman

le hall

le handicap

le hit-parade

le hold-up

le hooligan

l'interview (f.)

le jerry-can

le jogging

le joker (in cards)

le kidnapping

le kit

le knock-out

le label

le leader

le lifting (the facelift)

le living (= the living room)

le look

le magazine

le manager

le marketing

les mass-media (m.)

le music-hall

le must

le name-dropping

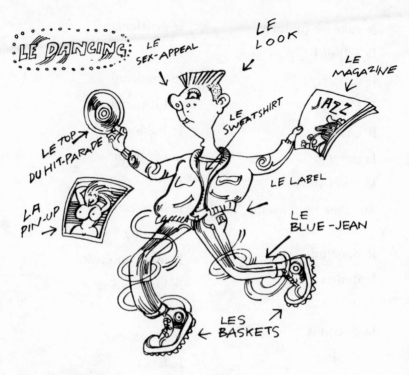

LE DANCING

LE SEX-APPEAL

LE LOOK

LE MAGAZINE

LE SWEATSHIRT

LE TOP DU HIT-PARADE

LA PIN-UP

LE LABEL

LE BLUE-JEAN

LES BASKETS

le one-man-show

l'outsider (m.) (in a race)

le pacemaker

le parking

le patchwork

le pickpocket

la pin-up

le planning

le playback

le play-boy

le pressing (= the dry cleaners)

le puzzle

le racket (the illegal one)

se relaxer

le scoop (journalistic)

la script-girl

select(e) (adj.)

le self-made-man

le self-service

le sex-appeal

sexy

le short (= shorts)

le show business

le sketch (in entertain-
ment)

le slogan

le snack (= snack bar)

snob

le software

le sponsoring

le spot publicitaire (=
the ad)

squattériser, le squat

le standing (= status)

la starlet, la star

le stock

le stop (= thumbing a lift,
hitchhiking)

stopper (to stop)

le stress

le studio (= one-room
apartment)

le supporter

le sweatshirt

le talkie-walkie (*sic*)

le time-sharing

le traveler's cheque

le week-end

These sentences should be no problem:

1. Le cover-story du magazine décrit le best-seller qui va faire partie du name-dropping littéraire aux dîners de Paris.

2. Le look de la saison est un véritable patchwork de styles.

3. Le sketch montrait des pickpockets dans un squat.

P.S. Add to the list most sporting terms, too numerous to be mentioned here (for example, le sprint, le tennis, le crawl, le recordman, le score, le match, and so on).

X
ALLONS ENFANTS:
Kids and kiddie talk

THE AU PAIR'S GUIDE TO KIDDIE TALK

"Mémé, le toutou, il m'a fait bobo." "Tonton m'a fait panpan parce que j'ai fait pipi dans mon dodo." Got it? If you're going to take care of the little brats, you'd better learn to communicate with them, so the following is required knowledge.

mémé	granny
pépé	grampa
tonton	uncle
tata	aunt
au dodo!	off to bed!
faire dodo	to sleep
le lolo	milk

le nounours	the teddy bear
avoir bobo	to have something that hurts ("**T**'as bobo à la papatte?" = Does your little leg/hand hurt?)
un bobo	a sore
la menotte	the hand
la papatte	the leg/the hand
les quenottes (f.)	the teeth
le toto	the head louse
le loulou	snot
le zizi	the genitals (male or female)
pipi (m.)	wee-wee, number one
caca (m.) / la grosse commission	poopie, number two
un prout	a fart
faire panpan	to smack
le toutou	the doggy
le joujou	the toy
faire joujou	to play
faire sisite	to sit down

To talk to small children in the idiotic way many adults do, simply repeat part or all of one-syllable words: "fifille," "chienchien," "papatte" . . . . Note that use of the above vocabulary is not confined to the kiddie community, as you may recall from previous chapters, where mention is made of "caca d'oie" and "métro-boulot-dodo." Many of these words also appear in satirical contexts, so to understand adult jokes, apply yourself to learning kiddie vocabulary.

"LE FRANÇAIS MÉPRISE LA JEUNESSE"

Jean Cocteau
Picasso
Editions Stock

Do Frogs like children? I am not terribly convinced they do. Before I get pelted with tomatoes by indignant Frogesses, could I simply ask you to draw your own conclusion from the large number of abusive terms used to describe children? Our "brats" is nothing compared with the variety of French names that have the same meaning but are too often used instead of "kids." For a start, even the normal words for "kids" (**"les gosses," "les mômes," "les gamins"**) are often preceded by "sales" (dirty; used here for lousy, rotten), which does not denote great tenderness. The following all mean "brats," have a note of unpleasant irony, can equally be preceded by "sales," and are quite commonly used:

les lardons (m.)

les mioches (m., f.)

les marmots (m.)

les mouflets, mouflettes

les rejetons (m.)

les moutards (m.)

les morveux (m., f.) (literally, the snot-nosed)

les chiards (m.) (literally, the crappers)

la marmaille (a group of noisy children)

Their native impatience prevents the French from putting themselves at children's level. They are easily irritated and can be very agile at distributing **"les claques,"** **"les gifles"** (slaps in the face). On the reverse side of the coin, the media often descend to maudlin, glutinous sentimentality, talking of "nos chérubins" or "nos petites têtes blondes" (they cannot be serious!). A final note, and conclude from it what you will: France has the second-worst record (after Hungary) for accidents in the home involving children.

XI
THE COCORICO SYNDROME:
Roosters rule ok

"Qu'est-ce que la France, je vous le demande? Un coq sur un fumier. Otez le fumier, le coq meurt." (What is France, I ask you? A rooster on a dung heap. Take away the dung, and the rooster dies.)

Jean Cocteau
La Difficulté d'être
Editions du Rocher

". . . forgive me, God,
That I do brag thus! This your air of France
Hath blown that vice in me."

Shakespeare
Henry V

It seems a strange idea, though perhaps an appropriate one, to have a rooster—that vain, strutting, loudmouthed, ridiculous creature—as a national symbol. Napoleon's eagle was certainly a more dignified idea, though he got his feathers plucked just as surely as the neighborhood barnyard rooster.

The Latin word *gallus* provides the symbol, "gallus" being at the same time "the Gaul" and "the rooster." No fools those Romans, they had already remarked upon the Gauls' loquacity as well as their querulous, aggressive nature. Tacitus reckoned that if the Gauls had stopped quarreling among themselves they would have been nearly invincible.

What other manifestations are there of what one could call the "cocorico syndrome"? Before I am accused of slander, allow me to point out that every year books are published in France analyzing and usually criticizing the French character and how it affects the individual's and the country's life; the French, given to self-analysis (**"le nombrilisme"** = navel contemplation), are quite aware of their defects and are sometimes even proud of them.

At the national level, the cocorico syndrome is revealed in the need to win acclaim, to have France's "destiny" and importance to the world recognized. It has made some Frenchmen say the most extraordinary things across the ages, such as:

"La gloire de la France est un des plus nobles ornements du monde." (France's glory is one of the world's most noble adornments.)

Montaigne

Mr. Supercocorico himself, General de Gaulle, was forever proclaiming France synonymous with grandeur and reckoned that she existed to "illuminate" the universe.

The press still talks of **"l'honneur de la France"** and sees failures or setbacks as humiliations. It is interesting to see how the "cocorico syndrome" has affected the French reading of history. Of course, each country has a selective memory for historical dates. Here are a few that are firmly imprinted on the national psyche, not all of them victorious moments either, though François Ier had a comforting word about that. Faced with defeat at Pavia, he exclaimed: "Tout est perdu fors l'honneur" (All is lost save honor) . . . to each his own priorities.

85

AD 52	Alésia: Vercingétorix, valiant leader of the Gauls, is beaten by the "sales" (i.e., rotten) Romans, who drag him back to Rome and execute him.
732	(Cocorico!) Charles Martel kicks out the "sales" Saracens at Poitiers.
1214	(Cocorico!) Philippe Auguste socks it to the "sales" league of English, Flemish and Germans at Bouvines.
1431	The "sales" English burn our girl, Jeanne d'Arc.
1515	(Cocorico!) François Ier socks it to the Swiss at Marignano.
1789	(Cocorico!) The French infuse the world with the spirit of liberty, equality, and fraternity.
1792	(Cocorico!) The people's army routs the foreign enemy at Valmy.
1870	Defeat at Sedan at the hands of the "sales Boches."
1898	The "sales" English humiliate us at Fashoda (Sudan).
1940	The "sales" Brits treacherously sink our fleet at Mers-el-Kebir.

At the individual level, we get "le Français frondeur" (antiauthority, ever critical), the opinionated, querulous, restless, contradictory undisciplined worshiper of speech who easily substitutes words for action. Shakespeare and Walpole knew a thing or two about "the confident and over-lusty French" (Shakespeare) and "their insolent and unfounded airs of superiority" (Walpole). Ah, now, speaking of lust, what of that worldwide, self-proclaimed reputation in this field?

The rooster makes a lot of noise and services many hens, but does he satisfy them? He obviously thinks so:

"Le Français est un mâle supérieur . . . comme
amant il crée partout." (The Frenchman is a superior
male . . . as a lover, he is ever creative.)

> Jules Michelet
> (nationalist historian 1798–1874)

"Le français . . . c'est la langue même des dieux, la
seule dans laquelle un homme puisse laisser entendre
à une femme qu'il l'aime." (French . . . is the very
language of the gods, the only one in which a man
can make a woman understand that he loves her.)

> Maurice Bedel
> (writer 1884–1954)

The Frenchman's ability in what he considers a sport and an
art form resides, as with his intellectual pursuits, more in form
than in content. Murmuring sweet poetic nothings that would
make anyone swoon with rapture is one of his prize talents
. . . yet what good is it to be told that one is a fellow's eternal
love when he omits to add "eternal love number 598"? To the
Frenchman, adultery is an accepted fact of life, and the
absence of extramarital pursuits might cast doubts on one's
virility.

Despite the leering, the coveting of the neighbor's wife and
the view of sex as proof of sporting prowess and artistic creativ-
ity, there are numerous maudlin articles in the press about
celebrities' fairytale loves. Nobody actually believes them but
everyone still reads the stuff.

The "cocorico syndrome" in its egocentric aspect produces
the legendary rudeness and the notorious shoving ahead of
one's place in line. A recent European poll is revealing: in a
list of seventeen qualities to be ranked in order of importance,
the French put manners in only tenth place.

Who says the French don't play much sport? It just depends
on one's definition of sport. The expression **"c'est tout un
sport"** has nothing to do with athletic pursuits; it refers to the
great effort necessary to accomplish something, as in "C'est

tout un sport de lui plaire" (It's very difficult to please him/her).

Recognized national sports are **"la resquille"** (getting something to which one has no right, getting away without paying for something; for example, fare evasion), **"la combine"** (scheming, beating the system, working around regulations for one's own benefit), and **"rouler le fisc"** (cheating on one's taxes). It follows from acceptance of these activities that the French are ever **"méfiants"** (distrustful, suspicious) and that one of their reflexes is to search for what might be concealed underneath an action or a proposal. The European values study showed that 71 percent of the French believe that people cannot be trusted. The rules of the aforementioned sports allow for **"la dénonciation"** (denunciation), a favorite French activity, along with its offshoot, calumny. Both make much use of the anonymous letter and reached their heyday under the German occupation in World War II.

The study also confirmed the importance of **"l'épargne"** (thrift). Indeed, the **"image d'Épinal"** (= stereotype; from the popular prints depicting typical scenes from French life, which came from Épinal from the eighteenth century onward) of the French includes the love of a good bargain (**"la bonne affaire"**) and an attachment to gold. There is a fortune of 4,500 tons of gold in private hands in France, as much as for the rest of Europe put together.

Speaking of gold, what are the gold-medal achievements of our fine-feathered friends, the **"cocoricorecords"** (a term coined by the magazine *Nouvel Observateur*)?

1. The second-highest alcohol intake in the world.

2. The highest rate of cirrhosis of all industrialized countries (our friend the liver strikes again).

3. The second-highest number of car accidents per head of population, a statistic not unrelated to the first record but by no means totally explained by it. The "cocorico syndrome" as it emerges in French driving habits deserves a special note.

A COCORICO NOTE: FROGS ON WHEELS

Be prepared: the French are selfish, macho drivers who tail-gate ("**coller aux fesses**"). They flash their headlights and honk their horns in an ever-present urge to overtake and speed away to the next traffic light. The women are as aggressive as the men, and the owners of small cars get orgasmic thrills out of overtaking more powerful Mercedes, BMWs, and the like. It might be useful to know some relevant vocabulary, and don't forget to perfect your "bras d'honneur" (see Chapter III). You will need it to express your indignation at nasty French driving. But since it requires the use of both hands, it might be better to teach it to your passengers so that, unlike the Frogs, you can keep your hands on the wheel.

un chauffard	a reckless, bad driver
faire une queue de poisson	to overtake and cut in close in front of the car you are overtaking (literally, to do a fishtail)
appuyer sur le champignon	to step on it, to put one's foot down on the accelerator (literally, to press down on the mushroom, from the shape of certain old-fashioned pedals)
conduire à la vitesse grand V	to drive at great speed, to go like a bat out of hell
brûler/griller le feu rouge	to go through a red light, to jump the lights

rentrer dans le décor

to drive off the road into a ditch, a tree, etc. (the consequence of the previous activities; "le décor" = the scenery)

se payer un arbre, un piéton

to drive right into a tree, to run over a pedestrian

cette bagnole bouffe de l'essence	this car is a gas-guzzler
c'est un vrai tape-cul	it's a bone-shaker (literally, it's a real ass-thumper)
un tacot un teuf-teuf	an old, slow-moving car
une bagnole poussive	a slow car
une contredanse un PV (un procès-verbal)	a ticket

It is worth knowing that French license plates ("**plaques minéralogiques**") give a clue to the driver's place of residence: the last two numbers correspond to his "département" or, in the case of Paris, to the city itself or its suburbs. The magic number is 75 ("ville de Paris") whose proud bearers can look in condescension on the Parisian suburbanites with their 78 (Yvelines), 91 (Essonne), 92 (Hauts-de-Seine), 93 (Seine-Saint-Denis), 94 (Val-de-Marne) and 95 (Val-d'Oise). All of these can in turn look down with pity or contempt on any other number. On the other hand, driving around the provinces with Parisian number plates can attract "**des remarques désobligeantes**" (unpleasant remarks) about "**ces sales Parigots**" (those Parisian bastards), given that their driving is even more selfish and aggressive than the national average.

Finally, if you want to be like the French, you may scoff at cars sporting the B sticker (Belgium) or the CH (Switzerland, or "cantons helvétiques") as the French love railing at these peoples' slow, clumsy driving.

XII
GEOGRAPHY À LA FRANÇAISE:
A linguistic study

PROFESSOR FRANCHOUILLARD'S*
GEOGRAPHY LESSON

Let's listen in to Professor Franchouillard's very own, very typical geography lesson on foreign countries.

Prof. Franchouillard: I shall tell you a joke. There once was a Belgian . . . hee, hee, ha, ha . . . (*He breaks into uncontrollable fits of laughter.*)

We, the audience: Are you all right?

Prof. Franchouillard: Yes, yes, ah mon dieu . . . There was once a Swiss . . (*More uncontrollable laughter.*)

Audience: Please, what can we do for you?

Prof. Franchouillard (regaining his composure): Listen, the English among you would say "There's this Irishman," the Americans would say "There's this Pole." Eh bien, nous, on

---

* Franchouillard = colloquial French for Frenchman, i.e., Frenchy.

dit "Y'a un Belge," "Y'a un Suisse," because the Belgians and the Swiss are so stupid, so thick, so slow! They have such funny accents! They say such funny things as "septante" (seventy) and "nonante" (ninety).

A *student*: Excuse me, sir, isn't it easier and more logical to say "septante" and "nonante" than "soixante-dix" and "quatre-vingt-dix"?

Prof. Franchouillard: Ta gueule ou je te fous mon pied au cul (shut up or you'll get a kick in the ass). Now, speaking as we were of those "sales Anglais," we and our language know how to deal with them! No need to remind you of **"filer à l'anglaise"** (to take French leave) and **"la capote anglaise"** (French letter). But do you know what **"avoir ses anglais"** or **"les Anglais débarquent"** (literally, the English have landed) mean? Ha, ha, ha, it means a woman's period has started!!! See in the image the suddenness of the flow of redcoats and the notion of invasion . . . brilliant, n'est-ce pas? As for **"le vice anglais,"** that's homosexuality (or, sometimes, flagellation), and **"anglaiser"** means to sodomize, to bugger . . . after all, we French know that the English are all fags. And such hypocrites! In their honor, we have the expression **"le coup de Trafalgar,"** which really means an unexpected catastrophe but is popularly used to mean an underhand trick, because the English are always playing dirty with their double-dealing, perfidious underhandedness. Anyway, we almost won Trafalgar and Waterloo, and we got that asshole Nelson!

A *student*: Have you any more world views to impart to us?

Prof. Franchouillard: If you have learned your lessons in our first textbook, *MERDE!*, you will know all about **"les Boches, les Amerloqs, les Ritals, les Rastaquouères, les Ruskis, les Bougnoules, les Bicots,"** and so on. As for our views on others, apart from the Belgians, the Swiss, and the English we're not all that bothered, except that, nowadays, we slavishly idolize everything American, all the while maintaining our belief in our own intellectual superiority. But we do have a few expressions that will come in handy:

une querelle d'Allemand	a quarrel started for no good or obvious reason (a throwback to the continuous and petty quarrels of the German princelings of old)
soûl comme un Polonais	blind drunk
avoir l'oeil américain	to have a sharp eye
c'est pas le Pérou	it's not a fortune, it's not a great deal of money, one won't get rich on that
une tête de Turc	a scapegoat, a whipping boy
fort comme un Turc	strong as a horse
le téléphone arabe	to spread a rumor by word of mouth
c'est de l'hébreu c'est du chinois	it's all Greek to me
les chinoiseries (f.)	1. unnecessary, hairsplitting complications 2. red tape
un casse-tête chinois	a real puzzle, a real headache
un supplice chinois	a cruel and refined torture, Chinese water-torture
boire en Suisse	to drink alone, in secret

point d'argent, point de Suisse	if there's no money to be had, there'll be no Swiss around
va te/allez vous faire voir chez les Grecs!	go get fucked! (cf. the ancient Greeks' homosexual leanings)

In contrast to the above, and quite rightly so, you should know that the word "français" appears in favorable expressions (Cocorico!):

en bon français	to put it simply
vous ne comprenez pas le français, non?	can't you understand when one speaks to you? (i.e., why are you so thick?)
impossible n'est pas français	the word "impossible" is not in the French language
une histoire gauloise	a dirty story, a risqué story

NOTES ON THE NATIVES

Everyone knows that there are two basic types of French people: the Parisians and all the rest, "les provinciaux," those poor second-class citizens given to staring incessantly and enviously at the bright center of all political, economic, cultural, financial, and educational life, all the while denouncing "le parisianisme" (the assumption that only Paris is deserving of one's attention). The stereotypical characteristics of the French are exaggerated in the Parisian, who adds to them a heavy dose of arrogance.

96

Two main forms of snobbery can be found in Paris (overlapping is possible), so let's have a look.

GALLUS LUTETIAE SNOBINARDUS
(Lutetia = Latin for Paris)

This is the moneyed and/or aristocratic branch.

HABITAT:
"Les beaux quartiers," which are basically the XVIe arrondissement, with some streets of the neighboring VIIIe, and some streets of the old VIe (Latin Quarter).

MIGRATORY PATTERN:
to the "château" or other "résidence secondaire."

DESIGNATION IN ORDER OF PREFERENCE:
1. A title, however bogus or "du côté gauche" (from the wrong side of the blanket, the term for titles conferred on the numerous illegitimate offspring of kings, princes, cardinals, and so on).

2. "La particule," the prized "de." These two letters, which originally meant nothing more than that their bearer came from a certain village, have acquired such an aura of grandeur that people search desperately for some ancestor who had such a "de," so that it can be tagged on to their own names. Or, if worse comes to worst, one can always insert it with impunity or change the spelling of one's name, just as Napoleon III's illegitimate half-brother, who was born Demorny, changed the spelling of his name to "de Morny" and called himself "duc"—so much more dignified.

3. A double-barreled name—and all the better if the barrels contain a "de," as in Madame de la Connerie de Merde.

4. Choice of first names. Exotic or medieval names set one aside from **"la populace," "le menu fretin," "le populo," "les gens communs,"** you know, ordinary people.

To demonstrate the above, let us examine the births, engagements, and marriages page of the *Figaro*, particularly on a Saturday. Take Saturday, 26 January 1985: on that day, "Le Carnet du Jour" listed twenty-three engagements, fourteen of which contained one or all of the previously mentioned assets. Example:

> Le vicomte Hugues de Monts de Savasse et la vicomtesse, née Chantal de Fournas de la Brosse, M. Yves du Mesnildot et Mme., née Marie de La Bourdonnaye, sont heureux d'annoncer les fiançailles de leurs enfants. . . .

As for the births section, exotic or medieval names given to the newborn were Typhanie, Apollonia, Colombe, Fleur, Solène, Amaury, Aliénor, Héloïse.

SPEECH:
The height of rarefied elegance, becoming thankfully very rare indeed, is attained by those parents who make their children address them by the formal pronoun "vous." It could result in "Maman, vous m'emmerdez!"

The tone of our "snobinardus" friend is not the braying of the English aristocracy but a more refined, slow, measured, assured tone of voice, delivery accompanied by the slight hooding of the eyes and an upward tilt of the nose. Useful long words to express one's amazement at another's vulgarity or stupidity:

d'une vulgarité, d'une bêtise	inénarrable	sidérante
	faramineuse	suffoquante
	monumentale	époustou-flante
	prodigieuse	hallucinante
	phénoménale	grotesque
	ineffable	aberrante
	inouïe	épouvantable

All give the notion of "extraordinary" and/or "breathtaking."

GALLUS LUTETIAE INTELLO-SNOBINARDUS

This creature can belong to the previous crowd, but its genus can exercise a tyrannical exclusivism all of its own. Its main weapon is manipulation of the spoken word, the more abstruse, pretentious, incomprehensible, and recondite, the better. The "snowing" of others to prove one's own intellectual superiority means being able to talk about everything with great assurance and to drown one's opponent in quotations, facts, and namedropping. Intellectual exclusivism is reinforced by the existence of "les grandes écoles," emergence from whose hallowed halls guarantees great prestige and often a viselike hold on the best jobs. Entrance by stiff competition only, please. The crème de la crème are the graduates of Normale Sup, l'ÉNA and l'X.

The ultimate intellectual hothouse is l'École Normale Supérieure, where the likes of Sartre, Malraux, and de Beauvoir, **"ont usé leurs fonds de culottes"** (wore out the seats of their trousers; that is, went to school). The end product is a **"normalien,"** and there ain't nothin' normal about those characters.

Know an **"énarque"?** He/she is a product of the highly competitive, postgraduate École Nationale d'Administration, a supertechnocrat with highly developed skills in the art of analyzing and dissecting (and not necessarily constructing) with tremendous command of language. He/she is destined for the high ranks of government service and is a readily identifiable, self-confident character.

What's the X? More reverence, please, l'X being not an unknown quantity but the very selective (intellectually speaking) École Polytechnique for engineering. Don't be put off by the polytechnic business; this is no second-class institution. One emerges with a passport to the upper reaches of the business world, full of theory and perhaps less so of practical knowledge, but that precious piece of paper precludes querying of one's ability. A **"polytechnicien"** makes a good marriage catch, as his earning power is pretty well guaranteed, unlike the aforementioned, whose involvement with the meaning of life, art and literature, or government service may not necessarily be rewarded in financial terms.

PROVINCIAL BRETHREN

Leaving Paris, what of the provincial brethren? Beyond the stereotype of the lumpen-provincial, there are regional variations: the "Marseillais" are considered liars and thieves, the "Corses" (Corsicans) lazy loudmouths, the "Alsaciens" Teutonic "bouffeurs de choucroûte" (sauerkraut-eaters), the "Basques" impetuous, and the "Bretons" thick.

The following commonly used expressions make use of certain accepted images:

faire une promesse de Gascon	to make an empty, vain promise
une histoire marseillaise	a tall story
répondre en normand	to answer evasively, non-committally
un(e) cousin(e) à la mode de Bretagne	a very distant cousin

A word on the "Normands": inhabitants of a rich, agricultural province noted for its butter, cream, and cheese, they are known particularly for their love of rich food. To help ingest gargantuan meals, rather than vomit "à la romaine," they devised **"le trou normand"** (the Norman hole). In the middle of a meal, one is given a glass of Calvados, the searing, local apple-based spirit whose function is to burn away previously downed dishes, thereby leaving more room—the "hole" in which to shove more food.

XIII
YOUR PH.D. EXAM

Armed with the knowledge gleaned from this book and from *MERDE!*, you must surely understand French better and more deeply than some jerkoff Ph.D. grind, so I have devised our own Ph.D. exam. Pass this one and, God forbid, you'll almost be a Frog! (Answers and translations on pages 103 and 104.)

Part A

"Les citations truquées" (falsified quotes). A few famous quotes have been tampered with. Where's the joke?

1. Je bande donc je suis. (René Descartes)

2. Le faim justifie les moyens. (Friedrich Nietzsche)

3. *Don Diègue*: Rodrigue, as-tu du coeur?
   Rodrigue: Non, j'ai du pique. (Pierre Corneille)

4. L'enfer, c'est les Parigots. (Jean-Paul Sartre)

Translate:

1. La reine Victoria: j'sais pas si son prince boche, Albert, était monté comme un âne mais, en tout cas, elle et lui, c'était du vrai lapinisme! Mais quand son Bébert a passé l'arme à gauche, elle en a eu gros sur la patate, elle a pleuré comme un veau et après, le zizi, c'était zéro pour la question. Ça s'appelle l'ère victorienne: "Le sexe? Nous, on est pas amusés!"

2. L'étranger de Camus est un drôle de zèbre. Sa vieille claque, il s'en bat l'oeil, il fait avaler son bulletin de naissance à un bicot; même quand il va se faire raccourcir, il s'en fout du quart comme du tiers.

3. La Tchécoslovaquie tapait dans l'oeil d'Hitler; il n'y est pas allé avec le dos de la cuiller, il se l'est payée. Les alliés n'ont pas remué le petit doigt. Chamberlain est même allé faire du lèche-cul et est revenu avec la déclaration de Munich qui ne valait pas un pet de lapin et où Hitler faisait des promesses de Gascon. Malgré tout, quand il est entré en Pologne, la moutarde est montée dans le nez des alliés et la guerre fut déclarée.

4. Les Franchouillards ont l'art de faire tout un plat de mecs désastreux: regardez Louis XIV et Napo, tous deux des mégalos à caractère de chien. Ils ont ramené leur fraise dans les affaires des autres pays, mais leurs idées de grandeur ont tourné au vinaigre. Un type qui s'est bien démerdé quand même c'est cette girafe de Gaulle, le gégène intello qui, même quand la France était sur les genoux, a fait des pieds et des mains pour continuer son one-man-show à Londres.

5. L'URSS mal léché, c'est Kroutchev battant sa table avec sa godasse.

Part A

1. The original is "Je pense donc je suis." But this version shows even greater proof of one's being alive ("bander" = to have an erection).

2. The translation of Nietzsche's "The end justifies the means" uses the French "la fin," but no doubt its homophone "la faim" (hunger) is an equally valid motive for action.

3. This is a classic schooldays joke. In *Le Cid*, the old geezer Don Diègue is slapped across the face by the father of his son's (Rodrigue's) fiancée (Chimène). He thinks it's a big deal, and in the scene whence comes the authentic quotation, he is about to ask Rodrigue to kill Chimène's dad (Don Gomès). He asks Rodrigue if he's got guts, or balls, or whatever ("as-tu du coeur?"). At school, instead of Corneille's answer, we all used to scream out "Non, j'ai du pique!", a "clever" play on the words for card suits ("du coeur" = hearts, and "du pique" = spades).

4. Sartre thought that hell was other people ("les autres"), but a vision of a hell made up only of Parisians ("Parigots") is terrifying enough.

Part B

1. Queen Victoria: I don't know if her kraut prince, Albert, was well hung, but anyway the pair of them bred like rabbits! But when her Bertie kicked the bucket, she was heartbroken. She cried her eyes out and after that, no more screwing. It's what's called the Victorian era: "Sex? We are not amused!"

2. Camus's stranger is a weirdo. His mom kicks the bucket, he doesn't give a damn, he does in some wog; even when he's going to the guillotine, he couldn't care less.

103

3. Czechoslovakia caught Hitler's fancy; he wasn't subtle about it, he just helped himself to the place. The allies didn't lift a finger. Chamberlain even went off to kiss some ass and came back with the Munich declaration which wasn't worth the paper it was written on and in which Hitler made promises he had no intention of keeping. Nonetheless, when he went into Poland, the allies got hot under the collar and war was declared.

4. Froggies love making a big deal out of losers: take Louis XIV and Boney, both ill-tempered megalomaniacs. They stuck their noses in other countries' business but their grandiose ideas went sour on them. On the other hand, one fellow who managed to do quite well was that beanpole de Gaulle, the intellectual general who, even when France was on her knees, moved heaven and earth to continue his one-man-show in London.

5. "L'URSS mal léché" is a pun on "l'ours mal léché" (= an uncouth fellow; literally a badly licked bear) which applies to the world-famous scene in which Khrushchev banged his shoe on a table while making a point at the United Nations.

Sheena realized she was getting hot. She felt drowsy, and a little dizzy, too.

And her head was starting to hurt.

Her stomach felt weird. She was starting to pant. . . .

Hold on a second. . . . Sheena stopped chewing at her toes. Was the nail polish making her sick? *Could this stuff be poison?*

Now Sheena's heart was pounding. She was panting heavily, but she couldn't get enough air into her lungs.

Would Amber know if nail polish was dangerous?

Could a puppy *die* from eating it?

Other books in the

ALL-AMERICAN PUPPIES ***Series by***

Susan Saunders

1: New Pup on the Block

2: On the Scent of Trouble

3: Camp Barkalot

Coming Soon

5: Puppysaurus

ALL-AMERICAN PUPPIES

4

UPTOWN POODLE, DOWNTOWN PUPS

Susan Saunders

Illustrated by Henry Cole

AVON BOOKS

An Imprint of HarperCollinsPublishers

CHAPTER ONE

"Are you watching me?" Sheena yapped at her four friends.

The dachshund puppy raced across her backyard to the first jump. She sailed neatly over the crossbar, her glossy reddish brown hair streaming out around her.

Sheena dashed to the plywood A-frame. She scrambled up to its peak, then hurried down the other side.

She leaped over the double bars of the next jump.

Without slowing, Sheena darted into the mouth of the yellow tunnel, zipped through it, and popped out.

She hurtled over another single jump, and sprinted to the teeter-totter.

The teeter-totter was the hardest part of the course. Sheena edged carefully up the narrow board until her weight tipped the far end downward. Then she trotted off easily and started running again.

Sheena dove through the center of the tire jump. She galloped to the back steps, where her four best friends were waiting.

"Now one of you guys do it!" Sheena said, breathless.

"Don't you think it'd be more fun if we all ran the course together?" Jake said.

Jake was a mostly black Lab puppy with four white feet and a white-tipped tail that hardly ever stopped wagging. He'd been living in the house across Sheena's back fence since Mr. Casey had adopted him from the animal shelter.

Sheena shook her head firmly. "No, it's meant to be used by one puppy at a time," she said.

"Maybe we could lay down secret scent trails," Tracker suggested. "Just to make things more interesting."

Tracker was a beagle puppy with long ears and the best nose in Buxton. His humans, the Pearsons, ran the Main Street Bakery.

"What's the point, anyhow?" said Rosie, frowning at the jumps.

A bristly gray puppy with funny-colored eyes, Rosie was born in the city. She lived with John now, the owner of John's Deli.

"It's supposed to be fun!" Sheena told her. "Plus Heather wants me to stay in shape."

Heather was Sheena's human. Heather's job was helping other humans exercise. When she decided she'd like to keep puppies fit, too, she built this course to try out on Sheena.

"I'd rather be chasing water rats at the lake," Rosie mumbled.

Fritz was the only puppy who hadn't voiced his opinion. He was the largest and strongest of the group, a German shepherd puppy with parents who were guard dogs. Not that it showed: Fritz was also the youngest, and he acted like a big baby lots of the time.

Since she lived right next door, Sheena always looked out for Fritz. Sometimes she was sure she could read his mind.

Hey, where is he anyway? Sheena wondered. *He was here just a second ago!*

Fritz wasn't sitting on the back steps any

longer. Sheena didn't see him anywhere in her yard, either.

Had something frightened him? Had he crawled under the side fence and gone home?

"Fritzie?" Sheena called out.

"I'm trapped in here!" came a muffled whine from Fritz. "Get me out!"

"He's in the tunnel!" Jake said.

"We're coming, Fritz!" Sheena said, hopping off the steps to help her friend.

The tunnel bulged where Fritz was stalled.

Sheena and Tracker squeezed into the near end of the tunnel, Jake and Rosie the other end.

"Walk forward, Fritz," Jake ordered. "Toward me."

"But I can't tell where I'm going!" Fritz groaned. "I don't know where you are."

"That's because there's a bend in the tunnel," Sheena explained. "Just ease around it and . . ."

"No way," said Fritz. "I'll get stuck in here

forever!" he howled. "I'll never see Greg and Marcia again!"

Greg and Marcia were Fritz's humans.

"You won't get stuck—*I* didn't!" Sheena said.

"I'm twice as big as you," Fritz pointed out.

"So back out, Fritz," Sheena directed. "One foot behind the other . . . that's right . . ."

Slowly the shepherd puppy edged out of the yellow tunnel. First his thick tail appeared, then each of his four legs, and finally his ears and his nose.

The puppy shook himself. "Whew!" Fritz murmured. "Thanks, Sheena—that was *scary.*"

"I have a great idea!" Rosie said suddenly. "Why don't we have a real race? Jake and I can start at one end of the course, and Sheena, you and Tracker and Fritz can start at the other end, and whoever finishes first . . ."

"Uh-uh, not me," Fritz said quickly. "I won't go into that tunnel."

"You can be the scorekeeper," Jake said to him.

"This course wasn't meant for a bunch of pups . . ." Sheena began to argue.

"I'll beat everybody!" Rosie said, taking her place on the far side of the tire jump.

"No way!" said Jake, lining up next to her.

"I'll bet I'm faster than both of you!" Tracker said, tail held high.

Sheena didn't want to be left out.

She hurried over to where Tracker was waiting, near the first jump, and stretched her leg muscles a couple of times.

"Okay, ready?" Fritz said from the back steps. "One . . . two . . . three . . . GO!"

Sheena and Tracker bounded over the first jump side by side, yapping excitedly, while Rosie and Jake took turns blasting through the tire jump, barking like mad.

The dachshund puppy and the beagle tried to climb over the A-frame at the same time. But in their rush they tripped each other up, toppling backward to the ground.

Sheena was the first to find her feet.

Meanwhile, Jake and Rosie were having problems on the teeter-totter.

Rosie had reached it first, with a few seconds to spare.

Then Jake jumped onto the teeter-totter as well, before Rosie was clear. He swung the gray puppy into the air, and she yelped nervously.

As soon as Jake inched forward, however, his weight sent the narrow board—with Rosie on the end of it—straight down to the ground with a thud.

The two of them bounced off the teeter-totter, cleared the single jump, and dashed into the tunnel.

Rosie was leading by a length.

Meanwhile, Sheena had clawed up and over the A-frame. She floated across the double jump and streaked into the opposite end of the tunnel. Tracker was only a step behind her.

Hanging onto her lead, Sheena barreled around the bend inside the tunnel . . . and smashed right into Rosie!

Tracker was moving too fast—he piled into Sheena before he could stop.

Jake went sprawling across the three of them, his tongue hanging out.

"Get off me!" Rosie growled from the bottom of the pile.

"Is anybody hurt in there?" Fritz asked worriedly from outside the tunnel. "Or stuck?"

Tracker yapped and wriggled backward.

Sheena's breath had been knocked out

of her, and her hair was rumpled, but otherwise she was fine.

Jake got hiccups.

And all at once four tails were wagging, and there were four toothy grins as the puppies tumbled out of the tunnel.

"That was great, wasn't it?" Rosie said, her eyes shining.

"Let's try it again!" said Jake, frisking around on the grass.

"I have the best time with you guys!" Sheena said. "Why don't we switch sides, and . . ."

Suddenly she heard Heather calling her, "Sheena? Sheena! Are you in the yard?"

"She's home for lunch early!" Sheena told the others.

None of the humans really knew much about the puppies' mornings together, and the puppies wanted to keep it that way.

"We're out of here," said Jake.

He and Rosie and Tracker scattered in three different directions, hightailing it for home.

Fritz was the last to leave.

When Heather opened the back door, she spotted the German shepherd puppy squeezing under his fence.

"You're getting too big for that, Fritzie," Heather said. "How would you like to have a bath, too? I've got some great new organic shampoo. . . ."

At the word "bath," Fritz gave an extra shove with his hind feet. He disappeared safely into his own yard.

But Sheena wasn't so lucky.

"I guess it's just the two of us, Sheena," Heather said to the dachsund puppy, gathering her up. "Would you rather have the oatmeal shampoo, or the avocado?"

CHAPTER TWO

Sheena hated baths.

It was embarrassing to be stuck in the kitchen sink with her long hair dangling around her like a wet rag mop.

"Just a couple of minutes longer, Sheena," Heather said. She squeezed some oatmeal shampoo into her hand. "Then I'll get out the hair dryer. . . ."

Sheena liked to look her best. She was proud of her glossy coat. But she'd had a bath a few afternoons ago, right? So why did she need this one? After a busy morning, she was ready for a snack and a nap.

"Somebody drooled on your ears,"

Heather was saying. "You've got a big streak of dirt down your back. . . ." She glopped more shampoo onto Sheena's shoulders. "I want you to look extra nice for Mrs. Vance and Amber," she added.

Who are Mrs. Vance and Amber? Sheena wondered. *Why do I have to look nice for them?*

"They just moved to Buxton," Heather went on as she raised peaks of lather on the unhappy dachshund. "Mrs. Vance wants Amber to meet a nice puppy to play with. And since I'll be working with Mrs. Vance every Tuesday and Friday . . . I thought I'd bring you along."

She rinsed Sheena well, turned off the faucet, and grabbed a fluffy towel. "Maybe Amber will use my agility course."

It's my *agility course,* Sheena thought grumpily while Heather blotted her with a towel. *Mine and Jake's and Tracker's and Rosie's. And Fritzie's.*

Sheena had to wait quietly while Heather combed her out and blew her

limp, dripping hair almost dry.

Then Heather fed her a half dozen peanut butter biscuits as a treat.

Heather hurriedly ate a cup of yogurt before loading the double jump, one of the single jumps, and the A-frame into her van.

She lifted Sheena onto the front seat and slid in next to her. They rolled up Liberty Lane, over to Main Street, and beyond. At last Heather steered the van between two stone gateposts. She followed a redbrick driveway to a large house built on the shore of the lake.

Sheena barked eagerly when she saw the water—she was picturing the fun she'd soon be having, chasing lake rats!

But Heather shushed her. "I have a feeling Amber isn't really used to other puppies," she warned. "Especially not rowdy ones."

Tucking Sheena under her arm, Heather pressed the front doorbell.

Ding-dong. Sheena could hear two sets of footsteps moving through the house. One was the tap of human shoes. The other was the click of puppy toenails.

The door swung open. . . .

"Ms. Seaford, come right in!" said a round lady with short yellow hair. "I'm Lillian Vance."

"Please call me Heather," Heather said. "And this is Sheena."

"Sheena, you're very pretty. This is my puppy, Tiffany's Amber Dream," Mrs. Vance said, bending toward the floor. "That's her

full name. But I simply call her Amber."

Puppy?

Sheena had never seen anything like what Mrs. Vance was scooping into her arms. It wasn't much larger than Sheena, but it was definitely fluffier. Small, bright eyes glittered in the center of a cloud of apricot-colored fluff.

Maybe it smelled like a puppy? Sheena sniffed the air . . . and sneezed.

Amber didn't smell like a dog at all—she smelled as though she'd been dipped in perfume!

Sheena sneezed again.

Mrs. Vance clutched the poodle puppy more tightly to herself and backed away.

"Sheena doesn't have a cold, does she?" Mrs. Vance asked Heather worriedly. "I've kept Amber away from other puppies because she's very sensitive to germs, and—"

"Sheena is healthy as a horse," Heather interrupted cheerfully. "Why don't we let

them get to know each other?"

She plopped Sheena down on the polished wood floor in the front hall.

"And we can take a look at that agility course I was telling you about," Heather said to Mrs. Vance. "I have part of it in my van."

"Well . . . if you're sure Sheena's not sick," Mrs. Vance said uneasily.

She set Amber down carefully several feet away from Sheena.

"Amber, sweetie, the patio doors are open," said Mrs. Vance, "so you can take this puppy outside if you want to."

The humans headed for the driveway, leaving the two puppies faced off in the hallway.

It was Amber's house—it was up to her to make the first move. But she just stood there, staring at Sheena.

"Hi," Sheena said at last, wagging her tail once or twice. She wondered if Amber had a tail to wag, hidden somewhere in that fluff.

"Hello," said the poodle puppy uncertainly. "What breed are you?"

"I'm a long-haired dachshund," said Sheena.

"I'm a registered miniature poodle," said Amber. "My grandmother won Best of Breed at the most important dog show in the country, and I plan to follow in her pawprints."

"I'm registered, too," Sheena said quickly. Amber didn't look as though she quite believed it.

"What do you do for fun?" Sheena asked her.

"Lillian and I watch television together on her bed," Amber said. "Sometimes we study dog show videos."

"I mean fun outdoors," Sheena said.

"We go for long rides in our car," Amber replied.

"What about when you hang out with other puppies?" Sheena wanted to know.

When Amber shrugged, Sheena said, "Do you have a yard?" She was losing hope.

"Of course I have a yard!" Amber said.

She led Sheena into a living room large enough for three couches. The apricot-colored poodle trotted across a rug softer than Sheena's best blanket, over to a pair of open doors.

"There it is," Amber said, stopping short at the threshold.

Bright green lawn stretched away from a stone patio until it met the dark blue of the lake.

This was more like it! "Water rats live around that lake," Sheena declared. "My friends and I have a great time chasing them. Want to try it?"

"Rats?" Amber shivered and danced away from the doors.

She's more of a baby than Fritz! Sheena thought.

That's when Heather walked around the side of the house. She was carrying the A-frame.

"You'll see how much Sheena enjoys this," Heather said over her shoulder to Mrs. Vance, who stood in the doorway next to the puppies. "I'm sure Amber will, too."

In just a few minutes, Heather had arranged the A-frame and two jumps in a triangle around an evergreen tree.

"Sheena, come on out here and show Mrs. Vance and Amber what you've learned," Heather said.

Sheena galloped across the patio to the grass, glad to have something to do.

Mrs. Vance watched with Amber in her arms while the dachshund puppy flew over the single jump.

Sheena scrambled up the A-frame and slid down the far side.

She cleared the double jump with room to spare.

Then she dashed over to Heather, who

was waiting near the evergreen.

"Way to go!" Heather said, clapping her hands. "See how much fun it is, Amber?"

Sheena was thinking: *Not nearly as much fun as it was when I was jumping with Jake and Tracker and Rosie.* She missed her friends.

Amber barely glanced at the jumps. Then she hid her fluffy head under Mrs. Vance's collar.

"That's all right, sweetums," Mrs. Vance murmured, and told Heather, "She's just not ready for anything quite so . . . active. She's still getting used to Sheena."

"Maybe next visit," Heather said, smoothing down the hair on Sheena's ears. "I'll leave the jumps where they are. Now we should begin *our* fitness program, Lillian."

CHAPTER THREE

Heather and Mrs. Vance headed upstairs to work out an exercise routine. Sheena wondered what she and Amber were supposed to do in the meantime.

The poodle puppy hopped onto one of the living-room couches and curled up in a ball. She was going to sleep the day away.

It was a beautiful, sunny afternoon, and Sheena didn't want to waste it. She trotted down to the lake.

There were rats, all right—plenty of them, living in holes along the shore. They had dark, greasy fur, slick pink tails, and lots of attitude.

They didn't run as quickly as rats did when Sheena was with her friends, even though she barked at them just as fiercely.

A couple of the larger rats snickered at her before they waded slowly out into the water.

When a huge rat whirled around and showed Sheena his dangerous-looking brown teeth, she retreated.

"I'll get you later!" she growled.

"Yeah? You and what army of puppies?" the rat sneered, and flicked his tail like a whip.

So Sheena sunned herself on the patio until Heather and Mrs. Vance finished exercising and came downstairs.

Mrs. Vance spotted Amber snoozing on the couch, and she whispered, "Poor little lamb—she's all worn out from entertaining her guest. Now when do we see you again, Heather? And Sheena?"

"Tomorrow morning," Heather said. "Bright and early. And every Tuesday and Friday morning after that."

Morning?

Sheena's heart almost stopped!

Mornings belonged to her and Jake and Tracker and Rosie and Fritz!

On the drive home, Heather murmured, "I believe Mrs. Vance waited a little too long to introduce Amber to other puppies—I don't think that poodle even realizes she's a dog. Playing with you twice a week will do her a world of good."

But Sheena was so upset that she hardly heard Heather. Was she really going to have to give her mornings up for that sissy little fuzzball?

Riding in the front seat of the van had always been one of Sheena's favorite treats. She was up high enough to see everything, and bark at whatever needed to be barked at: squirrels and birds and cats and dogs. But that afternoon she couldn't pay attention to the view. She didn't even remember to look for Tracker as they rolled past the Main Street Bakery.

Back at their house, Heather said, "You're going to be a big help to me at this new job."

She offered Sheena a cheese cracker.

But the dachshund puppy had no appetite. She let the cracker fall to the floor, uneaten. She plodded across the kitchen and slipped through the dog door. Sheena flopped down on the back steps, whining unhappily.

She hadn't been lying there very long when she heard the jingle of dog tags.

"Jake, is that you?" she barked hopefully.

"Me, and Waldo," Jake replied from across the fence.

Waldo was the cranky old sheepdog who lived with Jake and Mr. Casey.

"I'm coming over!" Sheena needed to talk to a friend.

She scrambled under the fence between her yard and Jake's. The black puppy ran to meet her as she popped out on his side.

"You don't look so good," Jake said.

"I'm *not* so good," Sheena said.

She told him all about Amber, ending with, "She didn't want to run Heather's course or chase water rats. She didn't even really want to go outside. What are poodles good for, anyhow?"

In a moment Sheena answered herself, "Nothing but sleeping on couches. And I have to give up our mornings for *her*?" she groaned.

Waldo was lying on his side in the shade of a tree, a mountain of gray and white fur. His eyes were completely covered by hair, and most of the time it was hard to tell whether he was awake or snoozing.

But suddenly he spoke.

"What kind of dog is she?" Waldo rumbled. "This puppy."

"A poodle," Sheena said.

"Poodles are water dogs," the old sheepdog said. "They're tremendous swimmers."

"No way!" said Sheena. "With all of that fluff?"

"That fur is to keep them warm in cold water," said Waldo. He added, "I knew a poodle once who was an excellent hunter and retriever."

"Like me?" said Jake, because he was almost all retriever himself.

"That's right—it's in their blood, just like it's in Jake's," Waldo said.

"Wow." Thoughts were spinning in Sheena's head. "So maybe Amber *could* act like a normal puppy after all," she said, "and chase rats, and swim, like us, and all she needs is a . . ."

". . . a shove in the right direction," said Jake.

"I don't know if I'm the right one to give it to her, though," said Sheena. "Amber didn't pay much attention to me."

"But she couldn't ignore all five of us," said Jake. "Where's Amber's house?"

"Way past the end of Main Street," Sheena said. "I'm not exactly certain where."

"If it's on the lake," said Jake, "Tracker and Rosie and Fritz and I can follow the shoreline until we find you. Easy."

Sheena was already feeling better. "Would you guys do that?" she said.

"Sure," Jake said. "We always spend our mornings together—why should that change?"

"You're going to get yourself into serious trouble, my boy, wandering the streets like a stray," Waldo grumbled at Jake from beneath the tree.

But Jake just wagged his white-tipped tail.

"I'll get Amber into the yard, if I have to pull her out of the house by her curls!" Sheena said.

CHAPTER FOUR

The next morning, Sheena didn't have to think of a way to get Amber outside.

Heather did it for her.

"Your puppy could use some fresh air," Heather told Mrs. Vance. They were drinking cups of herbal tea in the Vances' living room before starting their exercises.

"Amber *has* been a little droopy lately," Mrs. Vance said.

The poodle puppy was curled up next to her on one of the couches, nodding sleepily.

"I was afraid she might be coming down with something," Mrs. Vance added.

She glanced over at Sheena, sitting at

Heather's feet, and frowned as if she were still worried about the dachshund's sneezing.

"Nothing a little sunshine can't fix. Let's go, girls," Heather said to the puppies, opening the patio doors. She added, "Don't worry, Lillian—Sheena will look after Amber."

"Well . . ." Mrs. Vance was uncertain.

"If there's any kind of problem, Sheena will let us know. Pound for pound, she has the loudest bark in Buxton," Heather said. "Sheena, Amber—let's get you settled outdoors."

Mrs. Vance placed a couch cushion on the stone patio for her poodle.

"Amber doesn't like to lie on anything

hard," she explained.

When the humans walked back into the house, Heather pulled the doors closed behind them. So Amber was stuck outside, at least for a while.

"I'm going to run around the yard," Sheena told the poodle puppy. "Want to come with me?"

"I'd rather not—there could be fleas and ticks out there," Amber said.

She stepped daintily onto the couch cushion and lay down as close to the doors as she could.

Sheena cut across the lawn to sit at the edge of the grass. She cocked her head to listen. . . .

It wasn't long before she heard them over the lapping of the lake: Jake's mellow yodel, Tracker's long, drawn-out howl, Rosie's high-pitched yips . . . even Fritz's nervous yelp.

"They're all here. And they've found some water rats!" Sheena raced down the shoreline toward the racket.

Soon she saw her friends darting back and forth on the lakeshore. They were chasing the pesky rodents into holes, or pushing them out into the water.

"Hey, Sheena!" Jake barked when he spotted her. "This is a great place for rats!"

Rosie was tailing a large, brownish gray one, so she couldn't do much more than yip, "Hi-i-i!"

"We ran across some woodchucks, a raccoon, and . . . here's a rabbit!" Tracker yapped.

Nose to the ground, he followed a scent trail into a thick clump of weeds.

But Fritz hustled over to Sheena. "We're awfully far from our neighborhood," he whined.

"I know you are, Fritzie," Sheena told him. "But you're not lost—you can follow the lake to get home. And I'm so glad that you came."

"You're my best friend, Sheena," Fritz said, thumping her side with his thick tail.

When the three other puppies joined

them, Sheena said, "Amber's on the patio, sleeping."

"Mornings aren't for sleeping!" said Rosie.

"She has to see how real puppies act," said Tracker as they trotted along the edge of the lake. "We'll show her how much fun it can be to . . ."

". . . to swim, for instance," Jake added. The black puppy shook himself, flinging droplets of water everywhere—he'd already gone for a dip.

At the corner of Mrs. Vance's yard, Sheena warned, "Sssh—don't wake her yet."

She started across the lawn with her friends at her heels.

"But I don't see anybody," Rosie said. "Just a cushion. And a fake fur pillow."

"That's not a pillow—that's her!"

Sheena hissed.

"Amber? How could it be?" said Jake, puzzled. "Where's the head?"

"Where's the tail?" Fritz added, glancing back at his own long, feathery one.

Tracker was sniffing the air. "I smell . . . roses, or geraniums, and maybe some mint. Not a dog."

"I think it's her shampoo," Sheena said. "It makes me sneeze."

Amber didn't move at all until they reached the patio. Then the poodle puppy yawned, unrolling a pale pink tongue out of the cloud of apricot-colored fluff. Amber stretched . . . and opened her bright, round eyes. She saw them. . . .

She blinked.

Her eyes widened. . . .

"*Yi-i-ikes!*" The poodle squealed and scuttled backward toward the closed patio doors. "*A WOLF!*"

"It's okay, Amber!" Sheena barked at her. "These are my friends!"

"This isn't good," Fritz was moaning. "I knew it wouldn't be good!"

"*Attack dogs!*" Amber wailed. Had she never even *seen* any other kinds of puppies?

"They're here to meet you!" Sheena tried to explain.

But Amber was crying too loudly to hear her.

"Stop it—you're going to get us into trouble!" Sheena said, adding, "Guys, do something, quick, before the humans hear her!"

"Amber—watch this!" Tracker raced toward the single jump and bounded over it. "See how much fun this course is?" he barked enthusiastically to the poodle.

Amber was scratching desperately at the closed doors.

Jake took another tack.

"Amber, you're a poodle," the black puppy said sensibly, "so, whether you know it yet or not, you're good in water. And I'm good in water. Why don't we go down to the lake together, and . . ."

When he took one step onto the patio, however, Amber screeched as if he'd taken a bite out of her.

"Keep away from me! Help! Mommy!" she shrieked.

"'Mommy'?" Rosie repeated.

"She means Mrs. Vance!" Sheena said.

Bang! The patio doors flew open with a crash, and Mrs. Vance herself burst through them.

She took one look at Sheena's friends and screamed, "AMBER! UP!"

The ball of fluff sprang into her arms, sobbing wildly.

"Wherever did these . . . these hooligans come from?" Mrs. Vance yelled. "SHOO! SCOOT! I'm calling the police! The dogcatcher!"

That's when Heather hurried out of the house.

"Sheena, *sit!*" she ordered sternly.

The dachsund puppy planted her rear end on the patio.

Heather grabbed Rosie's collar with one hand, Jake's collar with the other.

"You don't have to call anybody, Lillian," she said. Heather hooked one of her legs around Tracker. "I know these puppies well," she added. "A couple of them are our

next-door neighbors."

"I don't understand. Why are they here?" said Mrs. Vance. "Did you bring them with you?"

"I certainly did not—I'm not sure *how* they got here. But I'll load them all into my van and take them straight home," Heather answered.

"Please do, the sooner the better!" Mrs. Vance said frostily. "Amber is frightened half to death—her poor little heart is pounding like a drum!"

Mrs. Vance backed toward the house, clutching her puppy to her chest. Neither she nor Amber took their eyes off Sheena and her four friends.

"Will I be working with you on Friday?" Heather asked her. "Same time?"

"I don't know!" Mrs. Vance huffed. "I'll have to wait until Amber gets over this awful shock—*if* she gets over it. I'm sure she'll need all of my attention for the next few days. She'll probably lose handfuls of her

beautiful hair from sheer stress!"

Safely inside, Mrs. Vance closed the patio doors and locked them.

"Thanks a lot, group," Heather said to the puppies gathered at her feet. "You've just lost me one very good job."

Still holding onto Rosie's and Jake's collars, she marched them around the house to the driveway.

Sheena, Tracker, and Fritz followed sheepishly.

Heather lifted each of the five puppies into the back of her van.

Then she loaded up the puppy jumps and the A-frame.

Heather climbed into the front seat herself and started the motor without another word.

"I'm really sorry, guys," Sheena murmured to the others as they rocked along the brick driveway to the road. "But at least we got our jumps back."

And our mornings, too.

CHAPTER FIVE

Or so Sheena thought.

But she couldn't have been more wrong. Things were worse than even Fritz might have imagined.

That evening, Heather got in touch with everybody's humans—Mr. Casey, Greg and Marcia, John, and the Pearsons.

She told them she'd found their puppies wandering far from home. And she suggested that they all take steps to keep it from ever happening again.

Sheena overheard Heather on the phone with Mr. Casey. "Jake could get hit by a car. Or someone could grab him off the street.

All of our puppies seem to be escape artists," Heather said, adding, "If Jake is going to be out in your backyard when you're not around, it might be a good idea to hook his leash to an overhead line."

The Pearsons decided Tracker should stay with them at the bakery all day long.

John said he would start taking Rosie to his deli.

Greg and Marcia weren't at home when Heather called, but she left a message for them on their answering machine.

"In all fairness, I think the other puppies lead Fritz astray," Heather said. "He's still just a baby. If Sheena and Jake are kept at home, Fritz probably won't be tempted to go anywhere alone."

Sheena would be locked in the kitchen when she wasn't on a job with Heather.

Before Heather left for work the next morning, she lined up Sheena's chew toys, her yellow ball, and some carrot chips near the puppy's pillow in the kitchen.

"I think that's everything you'll need, Sheena," Heather said. "I'll be back at lunchtime."

On her way to the van, Heather latched the dog door from the outside.

Sheena tested the door right away, shoving against it with her nose, and then with her front paws. It wouldn't budge.

So she was stuck in her house with nothing to do except listen to a very unhappy Jake.

The black-and-white puppy was outside his house, howling, "I'm chained to this tree like a . . . a dog! Fritz, are you there? I'll bet if both of us pulled on this chain, we could—"

"Uh-uh!" Fritz yapped from his own yard. "Greg and Marcia said if I don't stay put, they'll stick me at a dog-sitter's until I'm too old to wander!"

"You'd better settle down yourself, Jake!" Waldo rumbled. "Next stop for you could be the animal shelter!"

Now Fritz was whining, "I'm so-o-o alo-o-one. . . ."

"This is all my fault!" Sheena yelped

loudly. "If you hadn't come to help me—"

"I'd like to give that poodle a piece of my mind!" Jake barked.

"Put a lid on it, all of you—I'm trying to sleep!" Waldo growled.

As Sheena stretched out on her pillow, she was glad about one thing: She'd never have to see that ball of apricot fluff again.

Sheena slept most of the morning away, waking up when she heard the van rolling into the driveway.

"Hi, sweetie—how was your morning?" Heather asked the puppy as she stepped into the house.

Sheena's tail-wag was slow and sad, and Heather nodded. "I know," she said. "You're feeling crummy. I'm sorry you had to stay inside, but I won't have time to build you a pen until the weekend. How about a ride to the Main Street Bakery for a croissant? That should cheer you up."

Yes! The Pearsons' croissants were warm,

flaky, and delicious. Even better than that: Sheena might get to spend a few minutes with Tracker!

Her tail started to wag a mile a minute, and it kept wagging all the way to the bakery.

Heather and Sheena pulled into an empty parking space out front. And there the beagle puppy was, standing

in the door of the Main Street Bakery, keeping an eye on the street.

"Tracker!" Sheena yipped excitedly, hardly able to wait for Heather to lift her out of the van.

"Sheena!" the beagle puppy yapped.

He dashed down the steps to meet her. They touched noses and spun in circles, as though they hadn't seen each other in weeks instead of less than a day.

"Poor things," Mrs. Pearson said from the doorway of the store. "We're going to have to think of some way around this problem. Without the other puppies for company, Tracker is not himself at all."

Heather agreed. "Sheena is bored and groggy. . . . She doesn't even have much of an appetite."

Now that they were together, however, both puppies were starving. Sheena and Tracker gobbled down a half croissant apiece in a couple of seconds.

They were sharing a few more yummy

bites at the far end of the glass bakery case when someone called from the street, "Heather Seaford—is that you?"

The hair on the back of Sheena's neck stood straight up. "That sounds like Lillian Vance!" she muttered.

"I smell roses and geraniums," Tracker said darkly.

Sure enough, Mrs. Vance bustled into the store, carrying Amber in a large, open pocketbook. The poodle's fluffy head bobbed up and down with every step she took.

"What a wonderful place!" Mrs. Vance exclaimed. "Such mouthwatering smells!"

"Lillian Vance, this is Mrs. Pearson," Heather said. "Mrs. Pearson is one of the owners."

Mrs. Vance set the pocketbook on the floor at her feet and shook hands with Mrs. Pearson. Now Amber was eye to eye with Sheena and Tracker.

"Here comes more trouble," Tracker said.

Amber was staring straight at them. But this time she didn't wail or shriek.

The apricot poodle seemed to be gathering up her courage. After a couple of deep breaths, she hopped bravely out of the pocketbook. She paused for just a moment before taking a cautious step toward the puppies.

Something was moving on the far end of Amber's body. . . .

"Is she wagging her tail?" Sheena murmured to Tracker.

Tracker wagged his own tail in reply.

"I'm . . . I'm sorry I got you guys into trouble," the poodle began timidly. "But I'd never seen so many puppies . . . so many different kinds . . . at one time before, and I—"

"AMBER!" Mrs. Vance screamed suddenly, making Sheena, Tracker, and Amber all jump.

Before she could scoop Amber into her arms for safekeeping, though, Mrs. Pearson said, "Your puppy is just trying to make friends."

"Oh—do you think so?" Mrs. Vance said, straightening up.

"Amber seems glad to see them, Lillian," Heather said. "But we were just leaving, anyway. Come on, Sheena—let's get in the van."

Sheena gave Amber plenty of room on her way to the door. When she looked back, she was shocked: The poodle puppy and the beagle puppy were touching noses.

Sheena and Heather had errands to run. They shopped at Pet Paradise for puppy kibble and peanut butter biscuits, and they dropped off laundry at Snow White Cleaners. When they finally got back to their house, the red light was flashing on the answering machine in the kitchen.

Heather pushed a button and the machine

beeped. Then a voice announced, "Hello—Heather? This is Lillian Vance."

Sheena's ears pricked forward.

Mrs. Vance's voice went on, "I'd like to borrow Sheena if I could—for the afternoon? My little Amber Dream has been very listless, and their visit at the bakery seemed to cheer her up."

"Way to go, Sheena!" Heather said to the dachshund puppy.

"I'll take the two of them for a nice, long ride," Mrs. Vance's voice was saying. "We'll stop for some snacks along the way, and then I'll bring Sheena back to you before dinner."

Mrs. Vance cleared her throat, then added, "I *will* be continuing my fitness workouts with you. So if you'll call as soon as you hear this . . ."

"That's excellent news!" Heather said, and dialed Mrs. Vance's number.

"Hello? Lillian, this is Heather," she said. "Yes, your hour is still free on Fridays

and Tuesdays. . . . Of course you can have Sheena for the rest of the afternoon. I'll see you in a little while."

Heather hung up the phone and looked down at the dachshund puppy. "Take it easy, okay? Please try not to frighten Amber half to death."

CHAPTER SIX

Mrs. Vance drove a big car with dark windows.

Heather lifted Sheena into the front seat and set her down beside Amber.

"It's a much hotter day than I realized," Mrs. Vance was saying to Heather. "But I'll keep the air-conditioning on. . . ."

The poodle puppy was sitting directly across from an air vent, the cold breeze ruffling her curls.

"Be good," Heather whispered in Sheena's ear.

Then she waved good-bye, and Mrs. Vance backed out of the driveway.

"Hey," Amber said.

"Hey," said Sheena.

"Tracker's nice," the poodle added.

"*All* of my friends are nice," Sheena said firmly.

They glided past Fritz's house.

Sheena peered out the side window and wondered if the shepherd had heard her leaving. Now he really was alone, poor Fritzie.

They rolled around the corner.

Sheena spotted Puffy and Mr. Purr, the two fat orange cats from the Main Street Bakery. They were skulking around someone's front yard.

Puffy and Mr. Purr couldn't have seen Sheena, even if they hadn't been stalking a squirrel, because of the dark glass. But the puppies had always made a point of barking at the cats, just as the cats had always made a point of hissing at the puppies.

A deep, throaty *wooof* burst from Sheena's throat before she could stop it.

Of course the fat felines didn't hear her, not with the car windows rolled up tight.

But Amber jumped a foot into the air.

And Mrs. Vance exclaimed, "Oooh, Sheena—*please*! That hurts our ears, doesn't it, sweetums? You never bark, do you, my Amber?"

Sheena had heard Amber shriek and yelp and wail, but never bark.

"Why not?" she said to the poodle.

"I guess I've never had a reason," Amber said.

Mrs. Vance turned onto Main Street.

Sheena stood up on her hind legs to stare through the windshield as they moved closer and closer to the Main Street Bakery.

Would Tracker be hanging around out front?

Or was he snoozing in the back of the store?

The beagle puppy was nowhere in sight.

And the car sailed right past the Main Street Bakery without slowing down.

Sheena started to whine.

Mrs. Vance thought she was hungry.

"Let's not be greedy," Mrs. Vance said to Sheena. "We have a stop to make first. And then we'll think about treats."

A couple of blocks farther along, Mrs. Vance pulled into an empty parking space in front of Magic Touch Dog Grooming!

Another bath? Sheena couldn't believe her bad luck!

"Come along, girls," Mrs. Vance said, holding onto Amber and Sheena's leashes and opening her door. "I know you'll enjoy this."

For a split second, the dachshund puppy considered jerking her leash out of Mrs. Vance's hand. She could make a break for it, dash straight back to the bakery and hide with Tracker. Or maybe she could run all the way home and see Jake and Fritz.

Then Sheena remembered Heather's voice in her ear, asking her to be good. Besides, she felt kind of sorry for Amber.

Slowly, she followed Mrs. Vance and the poodle puppy onto the sidewalk.

But it wasn't baths that Mrs. Vance had in mind. She led the puppies right past the entrance to Magic Touch. She walked halfway down the block, to a shop with a hand painted on the window.

Sheena had never been here with Heather—it didn't seem to have anything to do with dogs. The front room of the shop was crowded with pairs of ladies sitting at little tables, their hands stretched out in front of them.

The air was filled with sharp smells.

Mrs. Vance told a large lady at a desk, "I'm here to have my nails done. And Nancy has agreed to paint my puppy's as well. I'm Mrs. Lillian Vance."

"Oh yes—come this way, Mrs. Vance."

The large lady dodged around women and tables. She showed Mrs. Vance and the puppies into a room at the back of the shop.

"Nancy will be right with you," she said.

Mrs. Vance sat down on a straight chair and lifted Amber into her lap. She started looking through a collection of tiny bottles lined up on the small table in front of her.

Sheena backed under a larger table in the corner. She didn't have any idea what might happen next, but she wouldn't have to wait long to find out.

A young woman with spiky red hair hurried into the room and said brightly,

"Good afternoon, Mrs. Vance. Who goes first? You, or your little dog?"

"Let's start with Amber," Mrs. Vance said, placing the poodle puppy on top of the small table.

Nancy opened a drawer and took out a nail clipper.

Heather cut Sheena's nails with a clipper—*click, click, click,* and it was done.

But after Nancy had clipped all of Amber's nails, she turned on a small, whirring tool about the size of a chew stick.

"I'm filing the edges of her nails smooth," Nancy explained to Mrs. Vance as she held the tool to each of Amber's toes.

Just listening to the buzzing sound made Sheena grit her teeth! She would have rocketed off the table if she were Amber.

The poodle stood quietly, staring straight ahead as if her feet belonged to another puppy altogether.

Maybe it's a show-dog kind of thing, Sheena thought. She could feel her own top lip

curling up angrily, however.

Then Mrs. Vance handed Nancy one of the little bottles. "'Very Berry Pink,'" she said with a pleased smile. "It's my favorite shade."

Nancy shook the bottle hard and unscrewed the top. She pulled a tiny brush out of the bottle. Carefully, she began to paint each of the poodle's sixteen toenails a bright pink.

Amber didn't so much as twitch a whisker.

But a growl was forming in Sheena's throat, and she scooted even farther under the table in the corner.

Finally Nancy was finished with the poodle puppy.

Amber's toenails glittered like little pink candies.

"Doesn't she look great?" Nancy said to Mrs. Vance, fluffing up the hair on Amber's head. "This polish, with her fur color . . ."

"Beautiful!" Mrs. Vance agreed. "Perfect. Let your nails dry before you do anything

lively, darling," she added, lifting Amber down to the floor.

"What about the other little dog?" Nancy glanced at Sheena, hunched under the table in the corner. "I think a dark red would be terrific with her reddish brown coloring. How about 'Madly Maroon'?"

"Well—I guess we could try," Mrs. Vance said uncertainly. "But be careful—I believe she has a temper."

"No problem."

Nancy tugged Sheena out of the corner by her leash. She plopped the dachshund down on the larger table before Sheena realized what was happening.

Nancy managed to paint only the four nails on Sheena's left hind foot. By then Sheena's lips had curled up so far that most of her sharp, white puppy teeth were showing.

"That's enough, Nancy," Mrs. Vance warned her nervously. "I'll put both puppies in the car, and I'll be right back to

have my own nails done."

"'Very Berry Pink'?" Nancy asked her.

"No, it's so hot this afternoon that 'Cranberry Ice' sounds more attractive," Mrs. Vance said.

She led Amber and Sheena toward the front door of the shop.

CHAPTER SEVEN

Mrs. Vance's car was sitting in bright sunlight—it had gotten as hot as an oven.

"I think I'll find a shady spot for you in the town parking lot," Mrs. Vance said to the puppies.

She plopped them down on the front seat and turned the air conditioning on high. She drove around to the empty parking lot behind the Main Street stores and pulled into a space under a big, leafy maple tree.

Mrs. Vance stayed with Sheena and Amber, the air conditioner running, until the car was nice and cool inside. Then she

turned the air conditioner off, rolled all four windows down just a fraction, and climbed out.

"Mommy will be back as soon as her nails are done, and we'll buy something scrumptious to eat," Mrs. Vance said to the poodle puppy. "Have a nice nap, sweetums. And you, too, Sheena."

She locked the car doors with her key and headed back toward the nail shop.

"How do you put up with all of this?" Sheena said to Amber as Mrs. Vance disappeared.

"All of what?" said the poodle puppy.

"Nail polish, for instance!" Sheena said to her. "What does nail polish do for a dog?"

"Mommy wants me to look my best," Amber said, curling up next to the steering wheel. "And it doesn't do me any harm."

"But you're missing out on so much puppy stuff!" Sheena said. "I'll bet you've never waded around in mud. Or rolled in

wet leaves. Or dug a hole with your nose.
Or . . . Amber?"

Amber's head was drooping closer and
closer to the seat. A few seconds later, she
was dozing.

"Well, *I* wouldn't stand for it!" Sheena

said, wrinkling her nose at her own dark red
toenails.

She got to work on them right away,
scraping polish off with her front teeth.

It took quite a while for her to clean
even one of her nails. Sheena realized she

was getting hot. She felt drowsy, and a little dizzy, too.

And her head was starting to hurt.

Her stomach felt weird. She was starting to pant. . . .

Hold on a second. . . . Sheena stopped chewing at her toes. Was the nail polish making her sick? *Could this stuff be poison?*

Now Sheena's heart was pounding. She was panting heavily, but she couldn't get enough air into her lungs.

Would Amber know if nail polish was dangerous?

Could a puppy *die* from eating it?

"Amber! Amber!" Sheena yapped, poking at the sleeping poodle with her unpainted front foot.

Amber seemed to have trouble raising her head from the car seat, and she was panting hard, too.

"*Umph?*" the poodle puppy mumbled. "Who? . . . Hard . . . to . . . breathe."

Was Amber sick herself?

Now Sheena's legs were wobbly, and her eyes felt heavy. . . .

She stumbled over to a window and barked as loudly as she could, "Help! We've been poisoned! We need to get to a veterinarian!"

Dr. Soboroff's office wasn't far away. Sheena could find it easily, if only she could escape from the car!

But the parking lot was still empty, and no one could hear her over on Main Street, not with the car windows almost closed.

Amber's sides were heaving, her mouth open, her tongue hanging out.

And Sheena was growing hotter and weaker and dizzier.

The dachshund puppy managed to hurl herself onto the dashboard. The sun had moved enough to shine through the windshield, and the dash was so hot that it scorched the bottom of her feet.

Sheena barked frantically. Then she half

jumped, half tumbled, onto the front seat again.

"You have to help, Amber!" she gasped. "Bark! As loud as you can."

The poodle forced herself to her feet, sucked in overheated air, and barked hoarsely.

Sheena scratched at the buttons in an arm rest, trying to open a window or door. But her legs gave way under her.

She felt herself falling . . . falling. . . . Her shoulder smacked against the floor of the car.

"We're done for," Sheena murmured breathlessly.

The last thing she heard was Amber, still barking.

Then everything went black.

Cool water poured down the sides of Sheena's face.

She tried to open her eyes, but the lids felt too heavy. . . .

Someone was barking furiously. . . .

It was a bark that Sheena knew very well!

"Fritzie?" she mumbled.

And Tracker—she'd recognize his howl anywhere.

Rosie was yipping, too.

Was Sheena dreaming? Or . . .

"She's coming around!" said a human voice. "Sheena?"

Sheena forced her eyelids up. One of Tracker's humans had found her! Mrs.

Pearson was dripping water onto her head with a sponge.

"Good! You're going to be fine, Sheena!" Mrs. Pearson said, dabbing at the dachshund's ears.

Sheena was lying on the ground under the maple tree, covered with cold, wet blue-and-white dish towels from the Main Street Bakery—they smelled a little like croissants.

"Keep those towels soaked," another voice directed—it sounded like Dr. Soboroff.

"Fritz, you can back away—we've got everything under control. You, too, Jake." Mr. Pearson was standing over Sheena with a worried-looking Tracker tucked under his arm. "Down, Fritz. *Rosie!*"

But Fritz, Rosie, and Jake stayed right where they were, their noses just inches away from Sheena.

"Amber?" Sheena rasped.

Before she got an answer, Mrs. Vance rushed up to them. "What is going on? Why

are these puppies out of the car?" she yelled. "And who broke my car window?"

"I broke it! And you're lucky that these puppies *are* here!" Mr. Pearson told her sternly. "Sheena and the other little dog would have been dead without them."

"'Other little dog' . . . Do you mean Amber?" Mrs. Vance shrieked. "Where is she?"

"The doctor's tending to her," said Mrs. Pearson.

Sheena raised her head to see Dr. Soboroff kneeling down on the far side of the maple tree. He was pouring ice water from a pitcher onto the towel-covered mound that was the poodle puppy.

"Is she . . . ?" Mrs. Vance began breathlessly.

"We don't know yet," Mrs. Pearson told her.

"But I don't understand what happened!" Mrs. Vance was crying.

"HEAT!" Mr. Pearson thundered. "Don't

you realize that a puppy can die in minutes in a closed car in the summertime?"

"But I parked it in the shade!" said Mrs. Vance, wringing her hands.

"The sun moves!" said Mr. Pearson. "And

when it's this hot outside . . ."

Jake and Rosie and Fritz were still checking out Sheena, and Mr. Pearson let Tracker take a closer look, too.

"Thanks, guys," Sheena said to them.

Four tails wagged so fast that they blurred.

"But how did you get here?" Sheena asked them. "How did you know I was in trouble?"

"I heard barking," Tracker said. "First you barked. Then you stopped, and a strange bark with sort of a yodel in it started up. . . ."

"Amber," Sheena said.

"I barked myself. . . ." Tracker went on.

"I heard him all the way over at the deli," Rosie told Sheena.

"And I was sitting on my back steps, feeling low, and all of a sudden I heard Rosie barking," said Fritz.

"Fritz helped me break my chain," said Jake—a couple of links dangled from his

collar. "We picked up Rosie at the deli. . . ."

"And Tracker had already raced out of the bakery to look for you," said Rosie.

"And the Pearsons came after me, and the other puppies. Mr. Pearson smashed the car window, and Mrs. Pearson called Dr. Soboroff," Tracker said.

"But you're okay," said Jake.

Fritz noticed Sheena's red toes peeking out from under the wet towels. "Your foot's bleeding!" he yelped.

"No, my toenails are painted," Sheena said. "It's a long story."

Suddenly Dr. Soboroff announced, "This poodle is going to make it."

And he told Mrs. Vance, "She is one lucky puppy to have good friends like these."

CHAPTER EIGHT

Two mornings later, Sheena, Fritz, Jake, Tracker, and Rosie were invited to a morning party at Mrs. Vance's house by the lake.

"A brunch for Amber's new friends," Mrs. Vance had said when she called Heather the night before.

There was great food, all of it home cooked by Mrs. Vance herself: peanut-butter-and-honey treats, cheese-and-bacon twists, chicken liver cookies.

There were games like Catch the Frisbee and Find the Tennis Ball.

There was an agility race, with Sheena,

Tracker, and Fritz on one team, and Rosie, Jake, and Amber on the other. Amber's team won, and Sheena didn't even mind, because the poodle was finally turning into a real puppy.

The six of them waded in the lake, they got wet and muddy, they chased water rats, they barked at ducks.

Amber promised Jake that she would let him teach her how to swim the next time they visited. "And when will that be?" she asked them.

"Every time Heather comes for a fitness

lesson: Tuesday and Friday mornings," Sheena answered. "Right, guys?"

"Right!" said her four friends.

Sheena knew there wouldn't be any problems in getting them to Mrs. Vance's: Heather would be happy to drive all of them in her van.

As she'd told the other humans, "It's clear to me that they're a lot safer together than they are apart!"

ALL-AMERICAN PUPPIES

5

PUPPYSAURUS
The pups dig up more than trouble this time!

Jake uncovers a giant bone while playing at the lake with his puppy friends. All he can think about is what fun he'll have gnawing on it. He sneaks it home and stashes it in the only safe place he can think of: the vegetable patch under Mr. Casey's prize pumpkin. When someone from the Natural History Museum hears about it and arrives at Mr. Casey's yard to investigate, though, the pups find out that perhaps their bone is more than just a big snack.